THE BEARERS OF BUSINESS LETTERS IN ROMAN EGYPT

ASSOCIATION ÉGYPTOLOGIQUE REINE ÉLISABETH

PAPYROLOGICA BRUXELLENSIA

Études de papyrologie et éditions de sources

publiées sous la direction de
Alain MARTIN & Paul HEILPORN

PAPYROLOGICA BRUXELLENSIA
— 41 —

THE BEARERS OF BUSINESS LETTERS IN ROMAN EGYPT

Paul SCHUBERT

ASSOCIATION ÉGYPTOLOGIQUE REINE ÉLISABETH
BRUXELLES

DIFFUSION : PEETERS
LEUVEN – PARIS – BRISTOL, CT

2021

ISBN 978-90-429-4730-6
eISBN 978-90-429-4731-3
D/2021/0602/186

Table of contents

Foreword

Business letters from Roman Egypt offer us a fascinating glimpse into the active life of ordinary people. At a time when transportation was slow, expensive and unreliable, the circulation of messages – short notes, orders, requests, letters of recommendation – could somehow mitigate the inconvenience created by the distance that separated individuals. The main purpose of business letters was to get things done. Presumably, the outcome was often successful, in spite of the frustration expressed by many writers who might as well have visited their correspondents if this had been practical.

In the absence of a postal service available to all, letters were placed in the hands of whoever happened to be travelling in the right direction. The bearer of the letter did not merely carry a slip of papyrus closed with a string and a seal: in many instances, he had to accomplish other tasks, such as delivering or collecting some goods, gathering information, or escorting a person.

This study of the bearers of business letters began with an attempt to map a typical structure of such documents. It soon became clear that the bearer, who frequently appears with an explicit mention in the text, plays an important role in the exchange. I thus found it necessary to consider more than the structural dimension, and to take into account the various aspects of his informal function.

For the most part, this fascicle was written during a research leave, which I received from the University of Geneva. I was able to continue my work during another leave funded by the Swiss National Science Foundation (grant # 174419). To both institutions, I wish to express my heartfelt gratitude for having shielded me from the bearers of many business letters: time for research, free from most administrative tasks and teaching duties, is a rare and valuable commodity.

1 Introduction

1.1 The bearer of a letter

The countless ancient letters written on papyrus and found in the sands of Egypt have been the topic of many scholarly studies. For the most part, the authors of such works have focused on the relationship between a sender and a recipient, and on the way by which virtual contact endures in spite of geographic distance; they have carefully examined the personal aspects of family letters, as opposed to business letters.[1] Less attention has been devoted to the bearer of a business letter, i.e. the person who carries the letter and delivers it.[2] The main purpose of this study will be to examine, relying on specific cases and examples, the role of the bearer of a business letter.[3]

1.2 Definition: business letters vs. family letters

Greek letters serve many purposes, all related to the need to communicate with someone living at a distance; they work as a replacement for direct conversation.[4] Business letters can be considered as a sub-group of a varied ensemble, which also includes messages with a literary dimension, official letters and correspondence between friends or family. The latter category displays some overlap with business letters because friends and family often conduct business together. In particular, the communication channels are similar; therefore, some details from family letters may be used to illustrate the way by which correspondence circulated in Roman Egypt.

In a family letter from a son to his mother, family matters are entangled with other elements that would rather suit a business letter.

---

[1] In particular Exler 1923; Koskenniemi 1956; White 1972.

[2] Some useful elements on the topic are to be found in Blumell 2014 : 46-53. He covers both family and business letters. Head 2009 also offers a good survey; it is devoted to letter-carriers explicitly presented as such, but rests on a corpus limited to the Oxyrhynchus papyri, and it does not distinguish family from business letters.

[3] All quotations from documentary papyri retain the original spelling, in most cases with a translation. I have corrected faulty spelling only when the quotation was incomprehensible. Unless stated otherwise, the translations of Greek passages are mine. In a few instances, a passage taken from papyri has been quoted twice, in different contexts, so as to spare the reader the effort of jumping back to a previous section.

[4] Koskenniemi 1956 : 38 – following ancient theory – underlines the role of the letter as a means to turn absence into presence; Ceccarelli 2013 : 2-10.

γ[ινώσκειν] ὑμᾶς θέλω ὅτι μετ̣[ὰ πάντων] ὁλοκληροῦμεν. θ[αυμάζω ὅ]πως καθ' ἑκάστην [ἡ]μέραν] ὑμεῖν γράφω κα[ὶ οὐδεμί]αν μοι ἐγράψατε. (...) κόμισον οὖν [. . . .] παρὰ τοῦ ἀναδιδοῦντι τ̣[αῦ]τά μου τὰ γράμματα ἀγ'γε̣ῖο̣ν̣ ἐλέου καὶ δὸς αὐτὸ Ἱέρακει, ἔχων ἐπιγραφὴν Ὥριων, ꝕ, καὶ πᾶν ποίησον ἐλθῖν πρὸς ἡμᾶς ἐν τάχι. ἐὰν δὲ εἰδῇς ὅτι παρὰ σοὶ μένι{ς}, ἀπόστιλόν μοι Θώνιον· αὐτοῦ γὰρ χρίαν ἔχω ἐνταῦθα.

I want you to know that we are well on all accounts. I am surprised that, although I write to you every day, you have sent me no reply. (...) Receive therefore (...) from the person who is delivering this writing of mine a jar of oil, and give it to Hierax – it has the inscription 'Horion' (ꝕ) – and do all you can to come to us quickly. If you see that he is staying at your place, send me Thonios; for I need him here.[5]

In another case, the sender also mixes family matters with some business: he sends his greetings to the recipient's children and wife, and then deals with a money deposit.

[ἀ]σπάζ[ομ]αί σε [δ]ιὰ Χ[. . . . .]ος τοῦ ἀναδιδ[ό]ν[το]ς σοι τ[ὸ ἐπιστ]όλιον καὶ τὰ ἀβάσκαντ[α παιδί]α καὶ τὴν σύνβιόν σου. (...) χάριν σοι ἔχω ὅτι ἐφρόντισας λαβὼν παρὰ Διονυσίου τὴν ἐπιθήκην, <ἣν> ἀπέσ[τει]λα τῷ Διονυσίῳ.

Through Ch(…), who is delivering this letter to you, I greet you as well as your children (may the evil eye spare them!) and your wife. (...) Thanks for having taken care to get the deposit from Dionysios; I had sent it to Dionysios.[6]

Family or personal matters can also be mixed with official duties. A *strategos* of the Sebennyte nome receives a letter from a person who seems to be his assistant. The bearer of the letter is carrying an ounce of purple dye, apparently as a present for the prefect's daughter.

ὡς ἠθέλησας, κύριε, τὴν οὐγκίαν τῆς πορφύρα[ς] ἔπεμψα διὰ τοῦ κομίσαντος [τ]ὸ ἀπὸ σοῦ ἐπιστόλιον φύλακος δοθησόμενον (l. -μένην) εἰς τὴν ξενίαν `τῆι μεικρᾷ´· σὲ γὰρ τῶι κρατίστωι ἡγεμόνι ἀκολουθεῖν ἐστοχασάμην.

As you requested, master, I sent the ounce of purple through the guard who brought your letter. (The purple) is to be given to the young one for the entertainment; for I guessed that you were in attendance with his excellency the prefect.[7]

Between business and family letters, there is a difference in the way the channels of communication are described in the letters themselves. In family letters, the sender frequently complains about the lack of reply from the recipient, and in such a context often mentions the name of a bearer. The rhetorical emphasis put on such claims, which serve also the purpose of showing how much the sender values a steady flow of communication with a

[5] P.Oxy. 14.1770.6-11 and 14-23 (late III AD). In P.Ryl. 2.242 (III AD), some family members are engaged in trade.

[6] P.Brem. 52.3-9 (II AD).

[7] P.Oxy. 6.931.3-9 (II AD). Conversely, instructions about forwarding an official letter from a manger to a *strategos* are imbedded in a soldier's letter; see P.Mich. 8.479.10-15 (early II AD).

friend or family member, somewhat undermines their credibility. Although not totally absent from business letters, those standard phrases seem to appear mostly in a family context; in a more matter-of-fact exchange, correspondents normally dispense with heavy displays of affection.

As a loose criterion, it could be said that business letters relate to professional, financial, logistical or commercial matters; also, in business letters, the main purpose is to get something done on the part of the recipient, whereas letters between family or friends often aim at sharing some reciprocal information about individuals. The typical clause where the bearer of a letter finds an explicit mention tends to appear most frequently in letters with a business content; in purely private matters, it is scarcer. Within a perspective where the bearer of the letter will hold the centre of the stage, we shall concentrate on exchanges where the sender expects the recipient to do something, frequently with the collaboration of the bearer.

Another reason for focusing on business letters is that they tend to display a more regular structure than in family letters. In such a structure, the bearer often appears explicitly, and we shall see that the relevant clause fits into a clear pattern. If one were to attempt a broad structural typology of private correspondence, business letters would offer a better potential for classification than family letters, where the attention of the writer often seems to drift at random.

1.3 Corpus

The corpus considered below will consist of Greek business letters, and also family letters that contain some elements of a business practice, from Egypt during the Principate. Although Greek business letters are to be found from the beginning of the Ptolemaic period till the Arab conquest, it will be convenient to focus mainly on documents from the first till the third century AD: at this time, letters are numerous and varied; in their structure and wording they display a consistency that allows for a clear definition of structure. A few examples from the early fourth century will occur when they seem relevant.

Identifying the relevant material within a mass of more than sixty thousand published documentary papyri is not an easy task. As we shall see below, the bearer of a letter is frequently mentioned with a standard wording, e.g. ὁ ἀναδιδούς σοι τὴν ἐπιστολήν 'the person who delivers this letter to you'. It is not enough, however, to search databases for a few standard expressions, especially since variation in spelling can be misleading.[8] In his study of letter-carriers with an explicit mention among the Oxyrhynchos Papyri, Head already noted that point: 'There was no standard terminology used for letter-carriers and

[8] E.g. ἀνδιδόντος for ἀναδιδόντος in PSI 13.1332.7 (= SB 5.7992; II/III AD).

therefore no way to collect examples of the role and function of (named) letter-carriers from straightforward computer searches (…).'[9]

Quite often, the bearer of a letter appears in an unconventional wording. Moreover, a faulty edition may conceal the words used for an automatic selection of sources.

> ἃ διέπεμψα ἐπιστόλεια ἔσχεν Ε̣ἰομίππος ὁ θεῖός σο[υ] παρὰ τοῦ κομίσαντος κα[ὶ] οὐκ ἂν ἐδοκεν **[correct *editio princeps* to οὐκ ἀνέδοκεν, i.e. ἀνεδωκεν]** μοι τ[ὰ γράμ]ματα Σω̣τ̣ίρας [.
>
> Your uncle Eiomippos received from the bearer the letter I had sent and he did not deliver Sotiras' writing (...).[10]

> ἔπεμψα διὰ τοῦ [ἐπιδιδόν]τος **[correct *editio princeps* to [ἀναδιδόν]τος]** σοι τὸ ἐπισ[τόλιον τ]υ̣ροὺς ξηροὺς λ (...).
>
> I have sent you through the person who is delivering this letter to you 30 dry cheeses (...).[11]

When the sender alludes to the dispatch of a letter, it does not necessarily imply that this is the one that was preserved to us.

> ἔπεμψά σοι ἐπιστολὴν διὰ τοῦ ἀρτοκόπου καὶ εἴσως οἶδας τί σοι ἔγραψα.
>
> I sent you a letter through the baker and perhaps you are aware of what I wrote to you.[12]

The sender is apparently alluding to a previous letter, to which the recipient did not give a satisfactory reply. We cannot be sure that the baker also carried this reminder.

It seems necessary, therefore, to follow a hybrid approach, where the material is sorted out in a broad fashion before a closer examination of the remainder can take place. Using the *Heidelberger Gesamtverzeichnis*, I selected all documentary papyri that carried the description 'Brief' (letter), within a time span from the first till the third century AD.[13] This yielded a rough corpus of ca. 2'000 documents, which had to be sorted out by a close reading of the text. After discarding official letters and other irrelevant material, and bearing in mind the imprecise and porous boundary between family and business letters, I was able to extract many details pertaining to the bearers of business letters. This was complemented with various other searches, as well as with information provided by other scholars who had worked on related topics.

Among the roles ascribed to the bearer of a business letter, the conveyance of goods is most frequent, as we shall see below. Quite often, a letter will mention the sending of wares, and

[9] Head 2009 : 282.

[10] P.Vars. 23.1-5 (II/III AD).

[11] P.Laur. 3.102 verso.10-12 (III AD).

[12] P.Tebt. 2.424.2-3 (III AD).

[13] <www.rzuser.uni-heidelberg.de/~gv0/gvz.html> 2059 hits on 27.07.2018.

we can suppose that they are being carried by the same person who is bringing the letter, although this is not clearly specified.

> ἔπεμψα δέ σοι διὰ Ὀννώφριος νε(ωτέρου) τὰ σύνεργα τῆς στολῆς τοῦ Ἡρακλείδ(ου) κρόκης μναῖ ζ ἐξ ὁλκῆς στατῆρε[ς .] . αἵ εἰ̣ς̣[ι] σύριγγες ρι καὶ στήμων ἀπὸ Λύκων πόλεως ὁλκῆς στατῆρες ϙ αἵ εἰσι σφαιρεία οε.
>
> I have sent to you by Onnophris the younger the yarn for weaving Herakleides' outfit: 7 *minai* of woof, weighing (...) *staters*, that is 100 reels; and warp from Lykopolis weighing 90 *staters*, that is 75 balls.[14]

The wording ἔπεμψα δέ σοι διὰ Ὀννώφριος 'I have sent to you by Onnophris' does not necessarily imply that Onnophris is also carrying the letter, although this is quite plausible. The presence of the bearer of a letter can thus be felt, but not ascertained. Conversely, in family letters, there are cases where the sender states explicitly that some announced goods have been travelling in the hands of another carrier.

> κόμισαι τὰ οἰκονομίδια ἀπηρτισμένα. ἔπεμψά σοι πρὸ τούτων διὰ Ὀσοράπιος ἱερέως τὴν οὐγκίαν τῆς πορφύρας καὶ πρὸ αὐτοῦ διὰ Πολυδεύκους βιβλία. περὶ ὧν δήλωσον.
>
> Herewith the documents, completed. Before these I sent you by the hand of Osarapis the priest, the ounce of purple, and before him books by the hand of Polydeuces. Let me know about them.[15]

> κόμισαι παρὰ τ[ο]ῦ ἀποδιδόντος σοι τὸ ἐπιστόλιον καλάθιον ἐν ᾧ ὃ ἐὰν εὑρίσκεις αὐτὸ ἀντιγράψις μοι. καὶ διὰ Οὐαλερίου τ[ο]ῦ χρυσοχ[ο]ῦ ἄλλο σοι ἀπέσ[τα]λκα.
>
> Receive, from the person who is delivering this letter to you, a basket; whatever you find in it, you will let me know in your reply. I have sent you another basket through Valerius the goldsmith.[16]

This can presumably be extended to business letters. Given the abundance of ambivalent sources, it seemed preferable to focus on letters where an explicit relation was made between the bearer of the letter and the goods he was carrying, or at least on cases where the context made the implicit presence of the bearer unmistakable. Finally, texts too damaged to yield any clear sense were omitted.

---

[14] P.Oxy. 31.2593.3-9 (II AD; transl. Rowlandson 1998 : 269).

[15] P.Oxy. 33.2679.4-12 (II AD; transl. P.J. Parsons).

[16] P.Mich. 8.481.5-10 (early II AD).

2 Parameters of letter delivery

2.1 Historical perspective on letter writing

Greek letters written in the Roman province of Egypt during the second and third centuries AD follow a practice that started several centuries earlier. It is possible to trace the form of letters to an earlier stage. Already in the *Iliad*, the hero Bellerophon becomes the first attested letter-bearer in Greek literature.[17] Letters become a regular feature in Greek literature in the sixth and fifth centuries;[18] and as a means of communication between distant partners – as opposed to a dialogue performed orally by heralds –, they find only limited acceptance before the fourth century.

On the material and structural side, early examples (sixth–fifth century) of letters written on lead and found in the Black Sea area do not display the division in three parts that will become the norm in the Hellenistic and Roman periods: a heading (where the sender and recipient are named), a central body (where the actual purpose of the letter is stated) and closing greetings.[19] Ancient tradition that attributes the first letter with the greeting χαίρειν to the Athenian general Cleon after the battle of Sphakteria (425 BC) is open to suspicion.[20] In a letter written on lead and found in Athens (late fifth / early fourth century), Ceccarelli identifies 'the exact transition between a narrative opening and a formal prescript'.

> Μνησίεργος ἐπέστειλε τοῖς οἴκοι χαίρειν καὶ ὑγιαίνειν.
>
> Mnesiergos sent to those at home greetings and good health.[21]

The shift to a formalised way of preparing letters takes place in Athens in the mid-fourth century, and the format is taken up by Hellenistic kings, who sent letters to cities.[22] It thus seems that Greek letters from Egypt preserved on papyrus are roughly structured in a way that was formalised elsewhere and earlier, but only by a few decades. The common use of the letter format in the documents from Ptolemaic and Roman Egypt mirrors the wide acceptance of letters in the Hellenistic world at large, as witnessed e.g. by the historian Polybius in the second century BC.[23]

---

[17] *Il.* 6.168-180.

[18] Ceccarelli 2013 : 35-47.

[19] Ceccarelli 2013 : 35-36, 40-41 and 56-57.

[20] Ceccarelli 2013 : 91-98.

[21] Ceccarelli 2013 : 45 and 352; SIG^3 3.1259.

[22] Ceccarelli 2013 : 266, 300 and 329.

[23] Ceccarelli 2013 : 167-178.

2.2 Delivery of letters

The imperial postal service (*cursus publicus*) carried messages – and sometimes goods or persons – for state service, but not for private purposes. The Roman army also offered, in some specific contexts, a network of messengers that served the needs of both the army and of civilian officials to carry letters and parcels, notably in the Egyptian Eastern Desert.[24] Messengers were either auxiliary horsemen or so-called μονομάχαι (or μονομάχοι).[25] For the civilian administration, the ἐπιστολαφόρος ('letter-carrier', also spelled ἐπιστολοφόρος) performed a public service (liturgy) in Roman Egypt, prolonging an office of the Ptolemaic administration.[26]

The delivery of official mail is illustrated by a letter to a *strategos* announcing the dispatch of letters and other documents.

> ὃ̣ν̣ δ̣ὲ λ̣έ̣γεις [μὴ κομίσασθαι ἀπόδε]σ̣μον ἐπιστολῶν προπεμφθέντα ὑπ' ἐμ̣ο̣ῦ ἔ̣τ̣ι ἀ̣π̣ὸ̣ [. . , ἐν ᾧι τοῦ κρατίστου] ἡ̣γεμόνος περὶ τοῦ ἐκκειμένου ἐν̣ [σι]τολ̣ό̣γοις [. . . . .] . . νω ἔκτοτε διαπεμψάμενος διὰ Κλαυδίου [. . . . .] ἔ̣δ̣ω̣κ(α) τοῖς κληρονόμ(οις) Ἰσχυρίωνος γενομ(ένου) βασιλικοῦ [. . . . . . . τὰ δὲ ἐπιστά]λ̣μ̣ατα Δημητριανοῦ ἱππέως τῷ̣ εἰς τὴν Β[α]σ̣ι̣λ̣ίου στατιῶνα ἐπιτηρητῇ̣, παρ' ᾧ̣ στοχάζομαι αὐτὸν μεμενηκέναι μὴ ὄντος ἐκεῖ τινος ἐπιστολαφόρου ἐκ τοῦ ὑπὸ σοὶ νομοῦ το̣ῦ̣ δ[ι]α̣κ̣ο̣[μ]ιοῦντός σοι αὐτὸν κατὰ τὰ κελευσθέντα. ὃν εἰ μέχρι νῦ̣ν̣ μὴ ἐ̣κ̣ο̣μ̣ί̣σ̣ω̣ι̣, φρόντισον εὐθέως πέμψαι τὸν λημψόμενον αὐ̣τόν.
>
> The packet of letters, which you say you have not received and which was previously sent by me as long ago as (...) including one from his highness the prefect concerning the decree issued to *sitologoi* (...), was then forwarded by me through Claudius (...) and given to the heirs of Ischyrion, former royal secretary (...), while the dispatches of Demetrianus, cavalryman, were given to the overseer at the station of Basilios, where I conjecture that the packet has remained, no messenger being there from your nome to carry it to you according to the orders. If you have not yet received it, take care to send somebody at once to take it.[27]

In this passage, the letters have been bundled together. The word ἀπόδε]σ̣μον was restored by the editors of the papyrus, but it finds parallels in the log-book of army messengers in the Eastern Desert, preserved on large *ostraka*.[28] Those document also indicate that, at least in the context of delivery through military messengers, they could be sent either sealed (ἐσφραγισμέναι), or open (λελυμέναι). For the public post, boxes or bags could also be

[24] Cuvigny 2005 : 5-7; Cuvigny 2019 : 70 thinks that this network of messengers maintained by the army in the desert does not correspond to a military postal system; rather, the army's presence in the desert provided the infrastructure that allowed the public postal system to function effectively in remote areas such as the Eastern Desert.

[25] Cuvigny 2019 : 78.

[26] Lewis 1997 : 28; on spelling, Kolb 2000 : 281-282; on the Ptolemaic office, Huss 2011 : 40-41.

[27] P.Ryl. 2.78.17-27 (AD 157; transl. adapted from the editors of the papyrus).

[28] Cuvigny 2019 : 80, quoting Vandorpe 1996 : 285.

closed with lead seals.[29] Given the haphazard nature of the informal communication of private letters, however, those were usually sealed.

The editors of another *ostrakon* tentatively read the presence of post-camels. They note, however, that the adjective ἀγγάριος 'of the mounted post' is not satisfactorily attested.

> προσδέχομαι τοὺς καμήλ̣ους ἀ̣γγαρίους ἕως ἐξέλθωσιν.
>
> I am waiting for the post-camels till they set off.[30]

In the absence of a public postal service available to all, letters were usually entrusted to a person who happened to be travelling along the desired route, or to a servant sent specifically to deliver the message.[31] Such attempts, however, were not always successful.

> καταπλέοντί μοι ε̣[ἰ]ς Ἀλεξάνδριαν διὰ σπουδῆς ἐγέ[ν]ετο γενέσθαι ε̣ἰς τὸ καταγώγιον τῶν ἀπὸ τῆς γεουχίας σου τὸ ἐν Μέμφει ἵνα ἐκεῖθεν σοι γράψω, καὶ οὐδένα εὗρον ἐρχόμενον πρὸς σέ.
>
> As I was sailing down towards Alexandria in haste, I happened to pass the lodgings located in Memphis (occupied by) the people from your estate, so that I might write to you, but I found no one who was going in your direction.[32]

2.3 Terminology

2.3.1 Words used for a letter

In the Greek world at large, the use of ἐπιστολή as a specific word for 'letter' appears in the fourth century BC;[33] it is abundantly attested in papyri from the Ptolemaic and Roman periods. Explicit reference to letters within the text of a letter itself occurs frequently, with the word ἐπιστολή and its diminutives ἐπιστόλιον and ἐπιστολίδιον hardly distinguishable.[34] A boundary between business and family letter is hard to perceive. The words γράμματα, χειρόγραφον and – for small slips of papyrus – πιττάκιον are also attested.

---

[29] Cuvigny 2019 : 81.

[30] O.Claud. 1.142.6-8 (ca. AD 109/100).

[31] Adams 2007 : 135–6 and 144; on the informal use of army patrols for mail delivery, 210; Blumell 2014 : 46-47. In P.Mich. 8.487.10 (family letter, II AD), a letter was apparently carried from Rome by a man called Eros, a name that would befit a slave. This letter works as an introduction and a request for an escort.

[32] P.Mich. 8.503.2-4 (late II AD).

[33] Ceccarelli 2013 : 18.

[34] Both ἐπιστολή and ἐπιστόλιον are ubiquitous; for ἐπιστολίδιον, e.g. P.Poethke 14.5-6 (II AD).

γράψον μοι ἐπιστολὴν διὰ τοῦ ἀναδιδόντος σοι τὸ ἐπιστόλιον.

Write a letter to me through the person who is delivering this letter to you.[35]

[τῷ ἀναδιδό]ṿτι σοι τὸ ἐπιστόλιον Θη[βα]ί[ῳ] δ̣[ὸς] (δραχμὰς) κδ ὀφειλομένας αὐτῷ.

To the Theban who is delivering this letter to you, give 24 *drachmai* that are owed to him.[36]

καλῶς ποιήσης, κύριέ μου, συνάρασθαι τῷ ἀναδιδούντί σοι τὰ γράμματα (...).

Please, master, help the person who is delivering this writing to you (...).[37]

(...) λημψόμενος παρ' αὐτοῦ τὸ χειρόγραφόν σου (...).

(...) when you receive from him the letter that is addressed to you (...).[38]

καλῶς ποιήσεις δοὺς τῷ ἀναδιδόντι σοι τὸ πιττάκιον Πασίωνι (...).

Please give to Pasion, who is delivering this ticket to you (...).[39]

The traditional distinction made between ἐπιστολή – where content takes precedence over the material dimension – and γράμματα – which emphasizes the visual aspect of the writing – does not seem relevant in the context of letters from Roman Egypt.[40]

2.3.2 *Words used to designate the bearer of a letter*

In the Ptolemaic period, the standard term used to designate a letter carrier is βυβλιαφόρος (or βιβλιαφόρος).[41] The bearer of a business letter, however, appears most often through the mention of ὁ ἀναδιδούς σοι τὴν ἐπιστολήν 'the person who delivers this letter to you', the grammatical case of the participle depending on the intended action. The participle ἀναδιδούς is by far the most frequently used form, at least in the early Roman period; this is also reflected in private letters of recommendation.[42] As early as the second century AD, but with increasing frequency till the fourth century, scribes display a tendency to retain in

[35] P.Oxy. 14.1757.19-21 (later than AD 138).

[36] P.Oxy. 59.3990.3-5 (II AD).

[37] P.Mich. 8.515 verso.1-2 (late III AD).

[38] P.Coll.Youtie 2.88.5-7 (IV AD).

[39] P.Gen. 1^2.2.1-2 (II/III AD).

[40] This general distinction was made by Ceccarelli 2013 : 18.

[41] Sarri 2018 : 18.

[42] Kim 1972 : 44-45.

the oblique cases the -ου- of the athematic nominative ἀναδιδούς, producing a hybrid ἀναδιδοῦντα etc.[43] The future participle is also used in a letter of introduction.[44]

Other verbs also appear occasionally, such as παραδίδωμι, κομίζω or καταφέρω (a late usage).

> ὁ παραδούς σοι ταῦτά μου τὰ γράμματα (...).
>
> The person who delivers to you this writing of mine (...).[45]

> δώσις δὲ τô κομίζωντί σοι τὴν ἐπισ{σ}τολήν (...).
>
> You will give (it) to the person who is bringing this letter to you (...).[46]

> Ἱέραξ (l. Ἱέρακι) οὖν τῷ [κατα]φέροντί σοι ταῦτά μου τὰ γράμματα (...).
>
> To Hierax, who is carrying to you this writing of mine (...).[47]

In private letters of recommendation, the following verbs are attested: ἀποδίδωμι, ἀναδίδωμι, κομίζω, παρακομίζω, φέρω, προσφέρω and καταφέρω.[48] The word ἐπιστολοφόρος, mentioned above in the context of a postal liturgy, also seems to apply to an ordinary letter-carrier in a family context. The sender being a soldier, however, it cannot be excluded that he resorted to some kind of informal help from a military messenger.

> εἶπέν [μοι] ἀναβὰς πρὸς ἐμὲ ὁ ἐπιστολοφόρος [ὅτ]ι ὅτε ἔμελλον ἐξελθεῖν εἶπον τῇ [γυν]αικὶ καὶ τῇ μητρὶ αὐτῆς ὅτι δότε [μοι] ἐπιστολὴν ἀπενεγκεῖν τῷ Πανίσ[κῳ] καὶ οὐ δεδώκασι.
>
> When the letter-carrier came up to me, he said: 'When I was about to leave, I said to your wife and to her mother: "Give me a letter to carry to Paniskos." And they did not give.'[49]

The vocabulary pertaining to letters is in no way restricted to business letters on papyri from the Roman period: it also appears in documents from the Ptolemaic period, as well as in Greek literary sources from various periods. The Zenon archive offers many instances of a standard phrasing where the bearer of a letter finds an explicit mention.

---

43 Mandilaras 1973 : 74, § 92.

44 P.Herm. 1.4-5 (I AD): Διόσκορον τὸν ἀ̣[ναδω]σοντί (l. -τα) σοι τὴν ἐπιστο̣[λήν].

45 P.Mich. 3.213.8-10 (III AD).

46 O.Claud. 1.171.8-10 (ca. AD 100-120); also P.Oxy. 6.936.13-14 (III AD).

47 P.Amh. 2.145.19-20 (late IV AD).

48 Kim 1972 : 43.

49 P.Mich. 3.217.20-25 (= SB 3.7249; AD 297).

καλῶς ἂν οὖν ποιήσαις δοὺς Νικάδαι τῶι τὰ γράμματά σοι ἀποδεδωκότι (δραχμὰς) ρν.
Please give 150 *drachmai* to Nikadas, who has delivered this writing to you.[50]

Ἀλέξανδρος ὁ ἀποδιδούς σοι τὴ[ν ἐπ]ιστολὴν τῶν φίλων τινὸς τῶν [ἐμ]ῶν ἐστὶν οἰκεῖος.
Alexandros, who is delivering this letter to you, is a close relative of one of my friends.[51]

ἀφεεστάλκαμεν Δεξίλαον πρὸς Ἀπολ[λώνιο]ν κομίζοντα ἐπιστολὴν περὶ ἀ[νηλωμάτων].
We have sent Dexilaos, who is carrying a letter about expenses.[52]

(...) συμπέμ[ψας μοι τό τάχος μετὰ] τοῦ ἀποδιδόντος σοι τὴν ἐπιστολὴν [τὴν τούτων τιμήν].
(…) sending quickly, together with the person who is delivering this letter to you, the price thereof.[53]

In literary sources, both the procedure and the wording seem to match what we can observe in papyri from Egypt.

τὸ δὲ χρυσίον τὸ λαμπρόν, ὅπερ ἔδωκας εἰς ἀποστολήν, ἄγει σοι Βακχεῖος ὁ τὴν ἐπιστολὴν φέρων.
As for the shiny gold which you gave for the journey, Baccheios, who is carrying this letter, is bringing it (back to you).[54]

οἱ δὲ παρὰ τοῦ Πτολεμαίου πρεσβευταὶ διαψευσθέντες τῆς συμμαχίας ἀνέδωκαν τοῖς ἄρχουσιν, ἑτοίμας ἔχοντες, ἐπιστολὰς παρὰ τῶν βασιλέων, δι' ὧν ἠξίουν (...).
The ambassadors sent by Ptolemy, cheated of the alliance, handed to the magistrates a letter from the king that they were holding ready in advance, by which they asked (…).[55]

πρῶτα μὲν ἐκέλευσεν ἀπὸ στόματος λέγειν τῷ Ἑζεκίᾳ τὰ ἐμφερόμενα τῇ γραφῇ, εἶτα καὶ αὐτὴν ἀναδιδόναι τὴν ἐπιστολήν.
First he ordered to communicate orally to Ezekias the contents of the written message, then to deliver the letter itself.[56]

This being said, documentary papyri from the Ptolemaic period and literary texts fall outside of the scope of the present study and will not be further examined.

---

[50] P.Cair.Zen. 1.59016.2-3 (259 BC).

[51] P.Cair.Zen. 1.59042.1-2 (ca. 257 BC).

[52] P.Cair.Zen. 1.59047.1-2 (257 BC).

[53] P.Cair.Zen. 1.59194.5-6 (ca. 255 BC).

[54] [Plat.] *Ep.* 1.309b-c.

[55] Pol. 29.25.7.

[56] Eus. *Comm. ad Is.* 2.12.

2.3.3 The bearer: explicit and implicit presence in business letters

The actual process of transmitting a letter requires the existence of a bearer in all cases, although there are instances where we must surmise his presence from the context. The following *ostrakon* offers an example of a complex transaction where the bearer appears only implicitly.

> Μάξιμος Ἰσιδώρῳ χ̣α̣ίρε̣ιν. ἰδοὺ μῆνες τρῖς ἐξ ὅτε ε̣ἴλ̣ηφας παρ’ ἐμοῦ (δραχμὰς) ιδ, οὐδὲ τόκον οὐδὲ [κε]φάλ̣ε̣όν μοι ἔδωκας. οὐκ ἔστιν εὔλογο̣ν̣ ἔμ̣ε̣ δανίζεσθαι, σοῦ μοι ὀφίλοντες (l. -τος). χρείαν̣ ο̣ὐκ ἔχω τοῦ τόκου. δόσι̣ς̣ οὖν Σερήνῳ τῷ φίλῳ μου στρατιώτῃ χορταρίῳ ὅ τι καὶ ἐγὼ ὀφίλω.
>
> Maximus to Isidoros, greetings. See, three months have passed since you received from me 14 *drachmai*, and you have given me neither interest nor capital. It does not make sense that I should be in debt while you owe me money; and I have no use of the interest. You will therefore give to my friend Serenus, a soldier in charge of fodder, what I myself owe him.[57]

The sender, Maximus, is claiming money back from Isidoros, the recipient; he asks him to repay this money to Serenus because he himself has borrowed from that person. This is a virtual payment, where the sender finds a shortcut and avoids one of the two payments that would balance the accounts.

Serenus is not explicitly described as the bearer of this potsherd, but several clues indicate that he is the person delivering the message to Isidoros. First, Serenus is presented as Maximus' friend (Σερήνῳ τῷ φίλῳ μου), which works as a kind of introduction for Isidoros; then Serenus' activity is specified – a soldier in charge of fodder – and Isidoros can check it if in doubt. Finally, this exchange finds a good parallel in a business letter where the bearer appears explicitly.

> Σύρος Ἀλεξάνδρῳ χαίρειν. καλῶς ποιήσεις δοὺς τῷ ἀναδιδόντι σοι τὸ πιττάκιον Πασίωνι ὑ(πὲρ) μὲν τόκου (δραχμὰς) δ (τετρώβολον) καὶ ἀπὸ τοῦ κεφαλαίου (δραχμὰς) δ, ὡς γενέσθαι (δραχμαὶ) η (τετρώβολον). ἀλλὰ μὴ ἀμελήσ̣ῃς, ἐπεὶ τὰς ἴσας ἔσχον παρ’ αὐτοῦ ἐνθάδε ἐπὶ τῆς πόλεως.
>
> Syros to Alexandros, greetings. Please give to Pasion, who is delivering this ticket to you, 4 *drachmai* and 4 *oboloi* as interest, and 4 *drachmai* from the capital, which makes 8 *drachmai* and 4 *oboloi*. Do not neglect the matter, for I have received the same amount from him here in town.[58]

Alexandros seems to be Syros' business partner. Pasion lent some money to Syros; Alexandros is to repay part of the debt to Pasion upon receiving this note. The document functions as a cheque and mentions explicitly the bearer's role and name. The parallel

---

[57] O.Claud. 2.266.1-7 (mid-II AD).

[58] P.Gen. 1^2.2 (II/III AD).

between the two documents presented above shows that the sender does not necessarily state explicitly the role of the letter bearer in a business letter.

A similar phenomenon occurs in the archive of Apollonios (*strategos* of the Apollonopolites Heptakomias in the period AD 113-120), where there are seven letters of recommendation.[59] Among those letters, two carry an explicit mention of the bearer as such.[60] The other five do not, although it seems almost certain that in each instance the person introduced to Apollonios is carrying the letter.[61]

Finally, circumstances can make the sender change his plans about the envisaged carrier.

> καλῶς ποιήσις δοὺς τὸ παρτικλάριόν μου ⟦υἱῷ Μέλανος προφήτου Πανοῦφι⟧ \`ἀναδιδόντι σοι τὸ πιττάκιον´.
>
> Please give this list (?) of mine ⟦to the son of Melas the prophet, (i.e.) Panouphis⟧ *correction above the line*: to the person who delivers this ticket.[62]

It seems that the sender had to adapt the dispatch of this letter after Melas' son was no longer available. Naming the bearer offered added security to the recipient, but this could backfire if the bearer turned out to be another person.

In sum, in many cases only the wording of the letter allows us to recognize the presence of the bearer in the letter. A list of books sent to the recipient, for instance, may provide a secure identifier.

> τὰ δὲ πεμφθέντα ἐστὶν δι' Ἀχιλλᾶ τὰ ὑποτεταγμένα.
>
> The (books) being sent through Achillas are those listed below.[63]

2.3.4 *Single or multiple bearers*

In most instances, the bearer is alone, but there are some exceptions.

> (...) τοῖς ἀναδιδοῦσί σοι ταῦτά μου τὰ γράμματα Διδύ[μ]ῳ καὶ τοῖς σὺν αὐτῷ.
>
> (...) to those who are delivering to you this writing of mine, Didymos and the persons accompanying him.[64]

---

[59] P.Brem. 5-9; P.Giss. 1.71 (= P.Giss.Apoll. 37); P.Giss. 1.88 (= P.Giss.Apoll. 41).

[60] P.Giss. 1.71 (= P.Giss.Apoll. 37) and P.Giss. 1.88.3-4 (= P.Giss.Apoll. 41).

[61] On the direct link between the letter of recommendation and the bearer, see also Blumell 2014 : 47, n. 70.

[62] SPP 22.61.5-6 (II/III AD). The παρτικλάριον is probably a list.

[63] P.Mil.Vogl. 1.11.8-9 (first half II AD).

[64] P.Flor. 2.258.3-5 (III AD).

The letter may be travelling along with a bulky delivery of goods, or even with a dead body, which easily justifies the presence of several bearers.

> εὖ ποι[ή]σεις τοῖς ἀναδιδοῦσι σοι ταῦ[τα] τ[ὰ] γ[ρά]μματα παραδοὺς μέτρῳ τῆς Τεπτύνεως κριθῆς ἀρτάβας τριακοσ[ί]ας (...).
>
> Please hand over to the persons who are delivering this writing to you three hundred *artabai* of barley using the measure of Tebtynis.[65]

> ἀξιώσω οὖν, κυρε μου, εἵνα δῷς αὐτοῖς γράμματα εἵνα μηδὶς ἐνοχλήσι αὐτοῖς καθ' ὁδόν, εἵνα δυνηθῶ κηδεύσας τὸ σωμάτιν ἐλθῖν πρὸς σέ.
>
> Therefore I ask you, my lord, to issue to them a written document so that no one will bother them along the way, so that I may bury the body and come to you.[66]

2.3.5 Gender

The conventional use of the masculine to designate a letter-bearer is made here by way of simplification. Judging from the grammatical usage followed by the senders, most bearers of letters seem to be male. Women nonetheless appear too, for example in a letter of recommendation sent to a *strategos* on behalf of a woman.

> Ἀπολλωνοῦν τὴν ἀναδιδοῦσάν σοι τὸ ἐπιστόλιον (...).
>
> Apollonous, who is delivering [feminine participle] this letter to you (…).[67]

In a chain of transmission of a letter, a woman can also receive a letter and forward it to the next person. The following case is particularly interesting, as it consists of instructions about the transmission of an official letter, embedded in the text of a private letter.

> ἀναδώσις Ταβαθεῦτι τὴν ἐπιστολὴν τὴν τοῦ διοικητοῦ πρὸς τὸν στρατηγόν. πᾶν δὲ ποισάτω ἀναδοῦναι αὐτὴν ταχύτερον τῷ στρατηγῷ ἵνα πρὸς τὰ γραφέντα αὐτῷ καὶ αὐτὸς ταχέως ἀντιγ[ρ]άψῃ.
>
> You will deliver to Tabatheus the *dioiketes*' letter for the *strategos*. Let her do her best so that she may deliver it with sufficient speed to the *strategos*, in order that he too may reply to what was written to him.[68]

---

[65] P.Mil.Vogl. 4.257.3-5 (AD 175).

[66] P.Oxy. 7.1068.23-27 (III AD).

[67] P.Giss. 1.88.3-4 (= P.Giss.Apoll. 41; AD 113-120).

[68] P.Mich. 8.479.10-15 (early II AD).

It is tempting to explain the scarcity of females in the role of letter-bearers by their reduced liberty of movement, in a society where women are often assigned to house-bound activities. We should nonetheless avoid being too dogmatic on this point. Women are known to travel in Egypt for family or business matters; in the latter case, they can be landowners.[69]

Women seem to carry letters also when they are directly involved in the business that appears in the letter. In one such case, a woman should collect the price for two *arourai* of land, presumably for a loan on security.

> ἡ φέρ̣ο̣υσά σοι Ταφόρσοις `Ὥρου´ ⟦απο παλωσεων⟧ `μητρ̣ὸ̣ς´ [Τ]α̣πα̣σίριος ἀπὸ Παλώσεως τ̣οῦτο τὸ ἐπιστόλ[ιο]ν πα̣ράσχου αὐτῇ ὑπὲρ ἀρου̣ρῶν δύο περὶ κώμην Νετρῶ ἀργυρίου δρα[χμ]ὰ̣ς πεντακοσία̣ς.
>
> The person who is carrying this letter is Taphorsois, daughter of Horos and Tapasiris, from Palosis. Provide her with five hundred silver *drachmai* for two arouras located near the village of Netro.[70]

In a family letter from a woman to another woman, the sender seizes the opportunity to write when a man is going downstream, but she also states her intention to go and visit a farmer herself; she seems quite able to travel on her own.

> Ἀχιλλᾶτος καταπλέοντος ἀναγκαῖον ἔγνων διὰ γραπτοῦ σε ἀσπάσασθαι. (...) ἐὰν αἱ ὁδοὶ στερεωθ[ῶσι] εὐθέως ἀπελεύσ̣ο̣μαι πρὸς τὸν γεωργόν σου καὶ αἰτήσω αὐτὸν τὰ ἐκφόριά σου.
>
> Since Achillas was travelling downstream, I assumed that I must greet you in writing. (...) When the roads become firm, I shall go off at once to your farmer and claim for you the rent from him.[71]

In another case, a man sends a letter to a woman through another woman, perhaps a slave, who is also carrying an order and some other items.

> λήμψ̣η παρὰ `Δόξης´ τῆς ἀναδιδούσης σοι τὸ ἐπιστολίδιον τὸ ἐντολικὸν Πτολεμαΐτος ὃ ἔλαβον παρὰ Χαιρή<μο>νος τοῦ ποικιλτοῦ πέμψαι αὐτῇ ὡς ἔδ[ω]κέν μοι ἐσφραγισμένον. (...) ἔχει πά̣λ̣ιν ἡ Δόξα ἄλλα `τινὰ´ ἃ ἔσχεν (...).
>
> You will receive from Doxa, the bearer of this note, the order for Ptolemaïs which I received from Chairemon the embroiderer, to send as he gave it to me, sealed. (...) Doxa has also other things which she received (...).[72]

---

[69] Bagnall & Cribiore 2006 : 81-83.

[70] P.Mert. 1.23.3-7 (late II AD).

[71] P.Oxy. 33.2680.3-5 and 10-13 (II/III AD); see Rowlandson 1998 : 235.

[72] P.Oxy. 14.1677.4-7 and 15 (III AD).

2.4 Conclusion

Business letters from Roman Egypt follow a regular wording, which allows both sender and recipient to recognize the basic elements that will frame the object of the letter itself. The bearer often finds explicit mention, but his existence does not require any special justification because the pattern of communication is well established among the inhabitants of the country. There seems to be no specific restriction on the choice of the bearer: whereas he normally acts alone, multiple bearers also occur; and although men constitute a majority among the bearers, women also play a role in the transmission of letters. Only children are never explicitly mentioned as the bearers of business letters.

3 Structure of communication in business letters

Identifying the bearer of a letter with a typical clause is a first step towards describing business letters in terms of structure. This approach is not new: previous scholars have attempted to conceive letter-writing in that way;[73] it will nonetheless be necessary to propose here a simpler model than what has been developed in the past, so as to focus more specifically on the role of the bearer.

In written correspondence, we can assume a minimal structure of communication where a sender passes a message on to a recipient. In many cases, however, the bearer of the letter plays an active role in the process: not only does he carry the document, but he also brings goods, money or information. It is thus possible to describe the structure of such letters in a dynamic way, where both the sender and the recipient have an interest at stake, and where the bearer usually becomes an instrument in the transaction.

I propose to define structural elements as blocks of text that display a standard wording and play a recognizable function. Business letters include structural elements that are essential (in most cases, they cannot be omitted from the letter) or optional (they appear in some letters, but not on a regular basis). The essential structural elements are: heading, required action, closing formula. An explicit mention of the bearer is not essential, but in the corpus under consideration, it occurs frequently.

> Ἐπώνυχος Ὥρωι [τῶι φιλτά]τωι ἀδελφῶι [χαίρειν.] δὸς τῷ ἀναδιδ[όντι σοι τὸ] ὄστρακον Κọλọ(φώνια) [̣] χρηστά. ἔρρωσο.
>
> Eponychos to his dearest brother Horos, greetings. Give to the bearer of this potsherd [figure lost] Colophonian vessels of good wine. Farewell.[74]

[73] In particular White 1972 : 1–41, whose description of letters found among non-literary papyri was in part biased by the second part of his study, on the Pauline letters in the New Testament.

[74] O.Stras. 1.792 (I BC / I AD).

An optional element can complement an essential element; the reverse is not true. Most of the structural elements go in pairs. Either those structural elements appear in a fixed relative position in the letter, or their position is loosely determined. Although a mention of the letter's bearer is optional, in the present context the focus of attention will be directed specifically towards this element.

The rules expressed here have a general validity, but they may suffer from exceptions. In some cases, the exceptions find a ready explanation, whereas sometimes we lack the precise contextual elements that might help us to understand them properly. Also, the labelling of some parts of a letter can be more problematic than it would appear at first glance because they can display an overlap of several functions.

structural element	*essential / optional*	*fixed relative position*
heading	essential	yes
(wishes of well-being)	optional	yes
context reminder	optional	yes
token of identification (σημεῖον)	optional	no
required action	essential	no
bearer (τῷ ἀναδιδόντι σοι)	optional	no
exhortation (μὴ ἀμελήσῃς)	optional	yes
justification	optional	yes
other business	optional	yes
communication to others (incl. greetings)	optional	yes
closing formula	essential	yes

3.1 Heading

The heading is one of the most stable elements in the structure of letters, at least from the fourth century BC till the fourth century AD. It requires no special clarification in the context of this study.

3.2 Wishes of well-being

In a letter where a bearer is explicitly mentioned, this clause appears only seldom, and mostly in the late third or in the fourth century.

> [προηγ]ουμένως εὔχομαί σε ὁλόκληρον ἀπολα[βεῖν καὶ τὸ] προσκύνημά σου ποιῶ καθ' ἑκάστην [ἡμέρ]αν παρὰ θεοῖς πᾶσι.
>
> First, I pray that I may find you in full health, and I prostrate myself on your behalf before all the gods every day.[75]

3.3 Context reminder

The sender often reminds the recipient of the general nature of the business under consideration.

> καθὼς παρα̣[τέ]θ̣ικά σοι τὼ μαρσίππιν̣ τ̣οῦ κέρματο̣ς̣, ἀπόδος αὐ[τ]ῷ̣ τῷ̣ ἀναδ[ι]δούντι [σοι] τ̣α̣ῦ̣τά μου τὰ γράμμ[ατα].
>
> As I have deposited with you the purse of money, give it to the person who delivers to you this writing of mine.[76]

> καὶ κατ' ὄψιν σε παρεκάλ̣[ε]σα ἕνεκα τῶν δέκα σταθμίων τῶν ἐ̣ρ̣ί[ων], ὅπ[ω]ς ἐν τάχει αὐτὰ ἀπαρτίσῃς.
>
> Already when we met face to face, I asked you about the ten loads of wool, so that you should have them ready.[77]

Besides recalling the context, this sentence also provides the recipient with a way of checking the sender's identity; the correspondents share a common knowledge of the setting. In P.Herm. 13, the sentences that follow the quoted passage indicate that the sender's concern lies elsewhere. He has already asked someone else to fetch the money, to no avail; he is now absent from home; and he is in need of his money.

This example shows that the boundary between the different sections of a letter is not always clear. The context reminder also plays to a certain extent the role of a token of identification, and one could argue that it carries a dimension of justification. In the following example, the context reminder is clear enough, so that we can grasp the outline of the story; but it also allows the recipient to ascertain the sender's identity.

---

[75] PSI 3.236.3-5 (III/IV AD); see also P.Oxy. 14.1770.4-6 (late III AD) and P.Oxy. 20.2275.2-3 (III/IV AD).

[76] P.Herm. 13.3-7 (IV AD); transl. adapted from the editor.

[77] SB 6.9160.3-7 (= P.Mil.Vogl. 3.201; II AD).

ἔδει μέν \`σε´ ⟦και⟧ χωρ[ὶς τ]οῦ με γεγραφέναι σοι διὰ Σαήτου ἀναπέμψαι τὰς (δραχμὰς) κ, εἰδὼς ὅτι αὐτόθι μετεβαλόμην τοῖς κοινωνοῖς μου αὐτάς, ἀλλὰ ἀνέμεινας τὸν τοσοῦτον χρόνον μὴ ἀποδούς.

You should have, without my writing to you through Saetas, sent me the 20 *drachmai*, for you know that I paid them here to my partners; but you waited all that time without paying me back.[78]

This section can be used simply to establish a communication that has been so far unsatisfactory.

3.4 Token of identification (σημεῖον)

Since letters sometimes had to be entrusted to strangers, communication between the sender and his recipient was hardly safe. In the following passage, the sender tries to reassure the recipient that he can trust the bearer of the letter and pay him the requested amount of money.

(...) λημψόμενος παρ' αὐτοῦ τὸ χειρόγραφόν σου μετὰ πάσης ἀσφαλείας (...).

(...) when you receive from him the letter that is addressed to you with all security (...).[79]

The sender merely states with some emphasis that this procedure is safe and that the bearer of the letter may be trusted. Another sender requires the transmission of a letter of credit through a safe channel.

τὸ ἐπιστόλιον τὸ τῆς ἐπιθήκης τὸ διαπεμφθέν σοι ἀπ' Ἀλεξανδρείας διὰ ἀσφαλοῦς μοι πέμψον.

Send me through a safe messenger the letter of credit that was sent to you from Alexandria.[80]

Sending letters of credit seems to be a particularly delicate task that requires great care in the dispatch. In the following example, the bearer is explicitly presented as someone in the direct service of the sender; moreover, he should be allowed to leave as fast as possible.

[78] P.Oxy. 3.532.2-9 (II AD).

[79] P.Coll.Youtie 2.88.5-8 (IV AD).

[80] P.Oxy. 41.2983.11-13 (II/III AD).

> ἔπενψά σοι Ἁρπουχρᾶν τὼν ἡμέτερον ὥπος λάβῃ παρά τοῦ ἀδελφοῦ μ̣ου γράμματα ἐπιθηκôν (...). ἀλ' ὥρα μὴ κατάσχῃς Ἁρποχρᾶν διὰ τὼ ἐπίγεσσθε περὶ τôν ἐπιθηκôν.
>
> I have sent you our man Harpokras so that he may collect some letters of credit from my brother (...). But make sure you do not keep back Harpokras because he is in a hurry on account of the credit.[81]

In other cases, however, the sender resorts to a sign of recognition, the function of which is to bring the recipient to trust the message's carrier. In the Classical period, this is called a σύμβολον and consists of two pieces from a single object – often a potsherd – that, by joining together, provide a proof of connection between two individuals. This device is also used in a metaphorical fashion, with the sender providing the recipient with a written token of identification.[82]

> ἀρχή σοι τῆς ἐπιστολῆς ἔστω καὶ ἅμα σύμβολον ὅτι παρ' ἐμοῦ ἐστιν· τοὺς Λοκρούς ποθ' ἑστιῶν νεανίσκους, πόρρω κατακείμενος ἀπ' ἐμοῦ, ἀνέστης παρ' ἐμὲ καὶ φιλοφρονούμενος εἶπες εὖ τι ῥῆμα ἔχον, ὡς (...).
>
> Let the beginning of this letter be for you at the same time a token that it is from me: one day, when you were entertaining the Locrian young men, you were seated away from me, and you got up to tell me, in a well-meaning way, a pleasant word, namely that (...).[83]

In papyri, this metaphor of a token is called a σημεῖον 'sign'. The σημεῖον clause constitutes the prototype of a password: in a fashion similar to Plato's σύμβολον, the sender is recognized by mentioning a piece of information that he and the recipient share in common (and that presumably the bearer cannot have made up).

> σημῆν (l. σημεῖον) ὅτι ἤκις καλῶν με καὶ τὸν γαμβρὸν καὶ λέγω σοι ὅτι ὀφθαλμιᾶ̣.
>
> The sign (of authentication) is that you came to call on me and (your?) son-in-law, and I told you that he was suffering from eye-disease.[84]

> (...) ἐπὶ σημέο̣ (l. σημείῳ) ὅτι σοι ἀφίοκα χοῦν ἐλαίου καὶ μάτιν πιπέρεος εἴνα παραδοῖς Καρίλα̣.
>
> (…) the sign (of authentication) being that I sent you a *chous* of oil and a *mation* of pepper to give to Karila.[85]

---

[81] P.Oxy. 51.3644.3-6 and 30-31 (III AD).

[82] Youtie 1970.

[83] [Plat.] *Ep.* 13.360a-b.

[84] O.Did. 361.6-8 (AD 76/77); transl. A. Bülow-Jocobsen.

[85] O.Did. 364.6-10 (discarded c. AD 88-96); transl. A. Bülow-Jocobsen.

σημείου χάριν ὅτι ἐνεβαλόμην σοὶ λινᾶ σέμεστα τριακοσία ὅτε ἐνέβης μετὰ Ἀλεξάνδρου τοῦ ὀθονιακοῦ.

As a sign (of authentification), (remember) that I loaded three hundred linen *semesta* when you embarked with Alexandros the linen-dealer.[86]

A σημεῖον clause appears also in the revised version of P.Prag. 1.111 (Appendix 1, below): it is a piece of information, not directly related to the business that constitutes the object of the letter, and presumably known only to the sender and the recipient, but not to someone who may want to forge or falsify the message.

3.5 Required action

The core element of the letter consists of the action required of the recipient: most often, he should give something to the bearer.

καλῶς ποιήσεις δοὺς (…) ὑ(πὲρ) μὲν τόκου (δραχμὰς) δ (τετρώβολον) καὶ ἀπὸ τοῦ κεφαλαίου (δραχμὰς) δ, ὡς γενέσθαι (δραχμαὶ) η (τετρώβολον).

Please give 4 *drachmai* and 4 *oboloi* as interest, and from the capital 4 *drachmai*, which makes a total of 8 *drachmai* and 4 *oboloi*.[87]

Apart from carrying the letter, the bearer can bring other items, collect some goods or money from the recipient, or he can perform an action for which he needs the help or protection of the recipient. This will be examined in greater detail below.

3.6 Bearer (τῷ ἀναδιδόντι σοι)

The bearer clause is normally associated with the description of the action required; it can be placed before, within or after the sentence describing the action.

καλῶς ποιήσις δοὺς τῷ ἀναδιδόντι σοι ταῦτά μου τά γράμματα (...).

[*required action*] Please give [bearer] to the person who delivers to you this writing of mine (…).[88]

In the phrasing of a single document, there can be a certain amount of variation, or even of repetition.

86 P.Oxy. 59.3979.13-14, with comm. and additional references. The nature of *semesta* (an *addendum lexicis*) remains unclear.

87 P.Gen. 1^2.2.2-4 (II/III AD).

88 P.Flor. 2.274.3-4 (AD 265).

(...) ἀποδοῦναι τὰ ἑκατὸν τάλαντα Δίῳ λημψόμενος παρ' αὐτοῦ τὸ χειρόγραφόν σου. (...) δοῦναι αὐτὰ Δίῳ τῷ ἀναδιδόντι σοι ταῦτά μου τὰ γράμματα.

(…) deliver the hundred *talanta* to Dios when you receive from him the letter sent to you. (…) give the (hundred *talanta*) to Dios, who is delivering this writing from me.[89]

The sender does not systematically name the bearer of the letter; but when he does, this constitutes a kind of introduction for the bearer. The sender can add some emphasis to this clause by placing it in the initial context reminder, as in the following example, where the sender underlines the parallel between a past context and a present request.

Χαιρήμονα τὸν ἀναδιδόντα σοι τὸ ἐπιστό[λι]ον τοῦτο οὐκ ἀγνοεῖς, ἄδελφε· καὶ γὰρ πέρυσι ἐπὶ τὴν παράλημψιν τῶν ἱματίων αὐτὸν παρὰ σοὶ κατέλειψα καὶ νῦν δὲ πρὸς παράλημψιν κρειθῆς ἔπεμψα αὐτόν (…).

Chairemon, who is delivering this letter to you, is not unknown to you, brother: for a year ago I left him with you for the collection of the coats; and now I have sent him for the collection of barley (…).[90]

In the following case, the bearer is not identified by name, but the parallel between past context and present request is very similar.

καὶ κατ' ὄψιν σε παρεκάλ̣[ε]σα (…) καὶ νῦν ἐ[ρω]τηθεὶς σπούδασον τῷ ἀναδιδόντι σοι τὸ ἐπιστόλιον αὐτὰ δ[ο]ῦναι (…).

Already when I saw you, I asked (…) and now, upon my request, take care to give them to the person who delivers this letter to you (…).[91]

3.7 Exhortation (μὴ ἀμελήσῃς)

Once the sender has requested an action, he may want to make his instructions more effective by insisting on the importance of the envisaged business. This is done by exhortation, often using a wording like μὴ ἀμελήσῃς 'do not neglect (the task)', or μὴ ἄλλως πράξῃς 'do not act otherwise'.[92] The clause replaces another, which was used in the Ptolemaic period, μὴ ἄλλως ποιήσεις (l. -σῃς) 'do not act otherwise'.[93]

[89] P.Coll.Youtie 2.88.3-7 and 15-17 (IV AD).

[90] P.Giss. 1.69.3-7 (AD 118/119).

[91] P.Mil.Vogl. 3.201.3 and 7-8 (II AD).

[92] Steen 1938 : 162-166.

[93] P.Heid. 7.393.5-7, with comm.

μὴ ἀμελήσῃς πολλάκις ὑπ᾽ ἐμοῦ περὶ τ[ο]ύτου παρακληθ[ε]ὶς καὶ εἰδὼς τὴν ἀνάγκην.

Do not neglect (the matter) for I have encouraged you often on this and you know how pressing it is.[94]

ὅρα οὖν μὴ ἄλλως πράξῃς.

See to it that you do not act otherwise.[95]

The sender may add some emphasis to his exhortation by repeating his entreaty, as for instance when he wishes to overcome the recipient's reluctance to send money.

(...) ἀλλ᾽ ὅρα μὴ ἀμελήσῃς ἀποδοῦναι αὐτῷ τὰ ἀργύρια [ὧν λήμψῃ τὸ] χειρόγραφ[όν σου]. (...) καὶ σὺ οὖν μὴ ἀμελήσῃς δοῦναι αὐτά. (...) μετάδος δὲ Δημητρίῳ ὅτι 'σπούδαζον πέμψαι τὰ ἀργύρια τοῦ ἀνθρώπου ἐπεὶ ἐπίτρ[ο]πος γέγον[ε]ν μὴ μ[ε]ταπεμφθῇς ὑπὸ στ[ρ]ατιωτῶν'.

(...) but make sure that you do not neglect to pay him the money for which you will receive the letter. (...) and you should therefore not neglect to give them. (...) Communicate also to Demetrios: 'Take care to send the money to the man now that he has become the middleman so as to avoid being summoned by soldiers.'[96]

περὶ τῆς παραγωγῆς τοῦ οἴνου μὴ ἀμελήσῃς (...) καὶ μελεσάτω σοι περὶ τῶν ἔργων.

Do not neglect to deliver the wine (...) and devote your care to this business.[97]

The sender defines quite precisely the role of the bearer of the letter: he is to collect some money from Demetrios (with the help of the letter's recipient) and bring it back to the sender. It seems that the recipient is under the threat of arrest; the sender obviously uses this circumstance to make him comply with the request. Threats occur in other letters.

ὅρα οὖν μὴ ἄλλως πράξῃς ⟦μὴ⟧ καὶ ποιήσῃς με πρὸς σὲ ἐλθεῖν συνζητήσοντά σοι.

See to it that you do not act otherwise lest you force me to come and look for you.[98]

In other parts of this letter, the sender's eagerness to get his money back is emphasised by his choice of words: ἀναγκαίως 'by necessity'; εὐθέως 'quickly'; ὅπως κἀμὲ ἄσκυλτον ποιήσῃς 'that you may save me too from trouble'. This presumably explains both the repetition found in P.Coll.Youtie 2.88 and the barely veiled threat that appears in P.Oxy. 3.532. It may also help to understand why, in the following instance, the sender embeds an exhortation within the required action.

---

[94] BGU 2.417.10-11 (II/III AD).

[95] P.Oxy. 3.532.15 (II AD).

[96] P.Coll.Youtie 2.88.8-9, 14-15 and 18-22.

[97] P.Tebt.Quen. 22.11-16 (II/III AD).

[98] P.Oxy. 3.532.15-18 (II AD).

ἵνα οὖν πέμψῃ<ς> μοι μίκκον χαρτάριον καὶ στημόνιν. μὴ ἀμελήσῃς. πέμψον μοι διὰ τοῦ ἀναδίδοντός σοι τὴν ἐπιστολήν.

(Ensure) that you send me the small slip of papyrus and the string. Do not neglect (the matter). Send it to me through the person who delivers this letter to you.[99]

3.8 Justification

An exhortation, however, may not be enough; the recipient is sometimes offered some kind of justification that again underlines the importance of the business.

(...) καὶ γὰρ ἐν Παώμει τότε σε εὗρον καὶ βουλόμενόν σε φιλανθρωπωσαι οὐκ ἀνέμεινας ὑπὸ κακοῦ συνειδότος κατεχόμενος.

(…) for the other day I found you in Paomis and wanted to treat you kindly; but you would not stay because you were oppressed by your bad conscience.[100]

The sender uses justification in order to strengthen his argument: the recipient will more readily comply with the request if he understands its urgency. In some cases, the justification actually tells quite an intricate story.

(...) ἐπιδὴ ὁ ἐπιστήκων Ἀνουβίων κατέχι αὐτὸν ὡς αὐτοῦ ἀποδράσαντος τῶν χρόνων Καστορίωνος. (...) εἶπέ μοι γὰρ ὅτι εἴ τι βούλεται διδῶ αὐτῷ, καὶ διὰ τοῦτο ἔγραψά σοι. ἐὰν γὰρ σὺ θελήσῃς, γείνεται αὐτοῦ τὸ ἔργον.

(…) since the superintendant Anoubion is holding him because he ran away in the times of Kastorion. (...) For he told me: 'If he wants something, I give it to him'. And for this reason I wrote to you. For if you wish so, his affair is concluded.[101]

This document does not imply a truly bi-directional business; it works more like a letter of recommendation. According to the sender, the bearer has the means to satisfy whatever wish the recipient may have. It thus seems that the bearer is trying to escape from Anoubion's grip and needs help from a person in a position of power, who will presumably act on the sender's recommendation.

3.9 Other business

The focus of a letter is not necessarily placed on a single issue. In the following example, the main point of the letter is to request some money; but the sender carries on with some additional information.

---

[99] O.Claud. 2.239.3-7 (mid-II AD).

[100] P.Oxy. 3.532.18-24 (II AD).

[101] P.Mich. 8.515.2-5 (late III AD).

περὶ δὲ τοῦ ἀδελ[φοῦ] Μέλανος τοῦ ξυστάρχου, περὶ τούτου πολλά μοι ἔγραψεν, ἀντέγραψα δὲ αὐτῷ πολλά. περὶ [μέν]τοι {περὶ} τῆς ἀποχῆς ἔγραψεν ὅτι ἀπὸ μέρο[υς ἔ]δωκεν Εὐδαίμονι, οὐκ' αὐτὸς μέν, ἀλλὰ ọ[ἱ εἰσ]ενεγ'κόντες ἐκεῖ τὰ ἀποσυστατικά.

As regards the brother of Melanos the president of the athletic association, he often wrote to me about the matter, and I sent him numerous replies. And concerning the receipt, he wrote that he gave it in part to Eudaimon, not himself, but those who brought there the introduction letter.[102]

3.10 Communication to others (incl. greetings)

A general mention of family relatives may appear, or of friends whose existence the sender wishes to acknowledge.

ἀσπάζομαι Σ̣ερῆνον τὸν ἀδελφὸν καὶ Πτολεμαῖον.

I send greetings to my brother Serenos and to Ptolemaios.[103]

3.11 Closing formula

The closing formula produces an echo to the initial heading. Here again, further elaboration does not seem necessary.

ἐρρῶσθαί σε εὔχομαι πολλοῖς χρόνοις.

I pray for your health over many years.[104]

3.12 Conclusion

Examination of business letters carrying a mention of the bearer reveals a structural pattern that fits not all, but most cases. To a core consisting of essential elements (heading, required action, closing formula), the writer adds various devices that will increase the effectiveness of an action in which he is only indirectly involved: the bearer, who is often mentioned explicitly, carries out the task assigned to him.

In this structure, two elements stand out because they underline a fundamental difficulty in the process of communication. First, a token of identification (σημεῖον) becomes necessary when the bearer's trustworthiness can be doubted by the recipient, as we shall see below in greater detail. In communication through letters, we witness only the written dimension of the exchange, but we have no idea of the oral communication that may have taken place, first between the sender and the bearer, then between the bearer and the recipient. Given

[102] PSI 3.236.15-20 (III/IV AD).

[103] P.Oxy. 59.3990.12-13 (II AD).

[104] P.Mich. 8.515.6-7 (late III AD).

the risk of distortion or abuse on the part of the bearer, the token of identification is an essential element of the exchange.

Second, the exhortation clause (μὴ ἀμελήσῃς) betrays another limitation induced by acting through a third party: the sender cannot necessarily count on the bearer to enforce the instruction as effectively as if he had appeared in person before the recipient. Therefore, the sender must make his presence felt as strongly as possible.

4 Various roles of the bearer

4.1 Delivering the letter to the proper address

The recipient of a letter normally has a given address, but this cannot be taken for granted: in some instances, the recipient is a moving target and the letter follows the tracks of someone who has departed elsewhere.

> εὐθέως παραγενάμενος ἐν Ἀλεξανδρείᾳ πρὸς τὸν Οὐαλεριν ἀπε͂λθα καὶ λέγουσί μ̣ο̣ι σήμερο̣ν̣ αὐτὸν ἐγδεδημηκ̣αίναι. ἔλαβαν τὸ ἐπ̣[ισ]τ̣όλιν ὡς ἵνα αὐτῷ πέμψωσ[ι εἰς] τ̣ὴν χώραν.
>
> As soon as I reached Alexandria, I went off to Valerius; and they tell me that he left today. They took the letter so as to send it to the countryside.[105]

Assuming that the address is stable, already in the Ptolemaic period, some letter-bearers receive written directions that will help them to find their destination.[106] Such directions also occur in the Roman period. In most cases, the sender writes them on the back of the letter, for the bearer to see.

> [ἀπόδος εἰς] Ἀλεξά(νδρειαν) εἰς Σεβα(στὴν) Ἀγορὰ(ν) ε[ἰς] τ̣[ὴν] . . . . . . .θήκην ὥστε Ἡρακλ(είδῃ) π(αρὰ) Σαραπίω(νος) . . . .ωνος το(ῦ) Σωσιπάτρου.
>
> Deliver to Alexandria, to Augustus' Market, to the (storing-place ?), for Herakleides, from Sarapion son of –on, grandson of Sosipatros.[107]

> εἰς τὸ γυμνάσι(ον) Θέωνι Νικοβούλ(ου) ἐλεοχρειστηι.
>
> To the gymnasium, for Theon son of Nikoboulos, municipal supplier of oil.[108]

---

[105] P.Oxy. 59.3988.3-9 (II AD [?]).

[106] P.Cair.Zen. 4.59653 (III BC).

[107] BGU 4.1079 verso.1-4 (AD 41).

[108] P.Oxy. 2.300 verso.12-13 (late I AD).

ἀπόδος ἰς τὸ Ἰσῖν Ἀπίωνι παστοφόρῳ παρὰ Θεονᾶτος.

Deliver to the Isis (temple), to Apion, priest, from Theonas.[109]

ἀπόδ(ος) Σενθῶνι ἐπὶ τῇ πλατείᾳ τοῦ θεάτρου παρὰ Γάιον (l. -ου) ἀπὸ Ὑπερηφάνου ἀδελ[φοῦ] κα̣σσιτερουργόν.

Deliver to Senthonis on the theatre square, from Gaius, tinker, on behalf of his brother Hyperephanes.[110]

In the third century AD, directions sometimes receive an explicit label: σημασία.

π(αρὰ) Ζώσιμος (l. -μου) Εὐφροσύν<ῳ> ἀδελφῷ σημασία· εἰς τὸ{ν} α μέρος Ἀντιν(όου) τῆς Ἑπτανομίας (...).
From Zosimos to his brother Euphrosynos, directions: to quarter # 1 of Antinoopolis, in the Heptanomia (...).[111]

ἀπόδ(ος) εἰς Ἀντινόου Σελβεινᾶτι π(αρὰ) Ἀθηνοδώρου στρατιώτου. σημ̣[ασί]α̣· ἀ̣πὸ βορρᾶ τοῦ ἱεροῦ τῶ̣ν̣ Ἑρμων[θ]ειτῶ̣ν̣ ἀντικρὺ τοῦ̣ [. . .]πωλ̣ί̣ου εἴσω εἰς τὸ ῥύμιον.

Deliver to Antinoopolis, to Silvinas, from Athenodoros, soldier. Directions: from the northern side of the temple of the Hermonthites, opposite the –store, towards the passage.[112]

Some sets of directions are prepared on a separate sheet of papyrus and contain detailed information, in the following case for delivery in Alexandria.[113]

Σημασία εἰς τὰ Βερνικειανοῦ ἄντικρυς τοῦ Ναναίου ὅπου τὸ Κλαυδειανοῦ βαλανῖον, νυνεὶ δέ ἐστιν ἡ οἰκία τῶν Ἰουλίων. ἐκεῖ ἐπιζήτησον Θεονάμμωνα γενόμενον γραμματ̣έ̣α Φωκίωνος, νυνὶ δὲ γραμματέως τῆς οὐσ[ία]ς αὐτοῦ.

Directions to get to the quarter of Berenikianos, opposite the Nanaion, where Claudianus' bath is located, presently there is the house of the Iulii. There look for Theonammon, former secretary of Phokion, who is currently secretary of his estate.[114]

---

[109] P.Oxy. 8.1155 verso.18-19 (AD 104).

[110] PSI 13.1331 verso.35-36 (III AD).

[111] P.Laur. 1.20 verso.2-3 (early III AD).

[112] P.Meyer 20 verso.3-5 (early III AD). Other examples in P.Oxy. 14.1678 verso.28-31 (III AD); P.Oxy. 14.1773 verso.40-44 (III AD); P.Hamb. 4.267 verso.2 (incorporating P.Ross.Georg. 3.6; ca. AD 336-348). In BGU 4.1064.18-19 (AD 277/278), the σημασία is apparently written at the bottom of the letter. SB 6.9126 is a mummy label, the address presumably attached to a coffin (see P.Par. 18bis = W.Chr. 499, III AD).

[113] Daniel 1984; Fowler 1985; Llewelyn 1994. For another striking example of directions for delivery in Alexandria, see P.Oxy. 34.2719 (late IV AD), interpreted by Gascou 2012.

[114] SB 16.12550 (III/IV AD).

4.2 Letter carrier

The bearer's first and most evident role is to carry a letter from a sender to a recipient. The sender can be away from home; or he is unable to perform an action and entrusts it to a messenger.

(...) ὅ̣τι ἐν ἀπ̣[οδη]μίᾳ̣ εἰμὶ καὶ οὐ δύναμ[αι ἐ]λ̣θεῖν ἐπ' αὐτά, χρ̣ίαν α̣ὐ̣[τῶ]ν ἔχων.

(...) because I am away from home and I cannot come and fetch (those items), although I need them.[115]

τῶι ἀναδιδόντι σοι ταῦτά μου τὰ γράμματα ποίησον αὐτὸν γεύσασθαι τοῦ οἴνου.

To the person who delivers this writing from me, make him taste the wine.[116]

Senders seize opportunities as they arise.

(...) τ[ῷ ἀν]αδι[δ]όντι σοι τὴν ἐπ[ισ]τολὴν ὀνόματι Σαραπίω(νι), ἐπ̣[εὶ εἰς Ἀ]λεξάνδρειαν πορεύετα̣[ι].

(...) to the person who delivers this letter to you – his name is Sarapion – since he is on his way to Alexandria.[117]

[ἐπέμψαμέν σοι ταύτην τὴν ἐπ]ιστολὴν διὰ τῶν φυλάκων [ἐκπορευομένων, ἐπειδὴ δι' ἄλλ]ου οὐ δυνάμεθα πένσαί σοι· (...) ἀλλὰ πάλ[ιν διὰ τῶν φυλάκων ἐπιστολὴν πέν]σον ἢ διὰ Πα̣ησ[ί]ου Πανβεῦτος.

We have sent you this letter through the police officers who were setting off, since we could not send it to you through anyone else (...). But in return, send a letter through the police officers or through Paesis son of Panbeus.[118]

καὶ δι' οὗ ἐὰν εὕρῃς ἐπιστολίδιόν μοι πέμψον.

And through anyone you may find, send me a letter.[119]

The bearer is expected to be a trustworthy person; depending on the additional business that he will conduct with the recipient, some degree of caution may be necessary. In the two following cases, the sender alludes to items other than a letter; but the process of transmission is similar.

---

[115] P.Herm. 13.10-12 (IV AD).

[116] P.Oxy. 12.1576.2-5 (III AD).

[117] SB 24.16339.7-10 (= P.Harr. 1.153; III AD).

[118] P.Iand. 2.10.2-5 (III AD).

[119] P.Ross.Georg. 3.3.13-14 (= SB 3.7242; III AD).

ἠὰν εὕρω τεινὰ πειστὸν πέμψω.

When I find someone trustworthy, I shall send (the requested *chiton*).[120]

ἐπεθέμην Σαραπίων[ι] τῶ`ι´ ἀδελφῶι ἵνα ὅσα ἐὰν ἔχῃς μοι πέμψαι ἀσφαλῶς δι᾽ αὐτοῦ πεμφθῆι.

I imposed on my brother Sarapion that, whatever you may have to send to me, be sent securely through him.[121]

The sender of another letter refers to τῷ παρὰ σοῦ 'the person coming from [the recipient]', then makes an explicit statement on the bearer's behaviour.

ὅρα μή σε παραλογείσειται {σε}, ὡς κοινῶς ἠγορακέναι παραλελόγισται.

Ensure that he does not cheat on you, since it has been common practice for him to cheat in the buying process.[122]

In another case already mentioned above, the sender has asked the recipient for what looks like a list (τὸ παρτικλάριόν μου), then adds that it should be sealed before sending (ἐσφραγισμένον πέμψις μοι), presumably to keep it confidential.[123] The bearer's negligence also appears to undermine the sender's credit.

ἡ τῶν παρακομισζόντων (l. -μιζ-) ἀμέλεια διέβαλεν ἡμᾶς ὡς ἀμελεῖς.

The negligence of those who carry (the letters) has given the false impression that we were negligent.[124]

Double-checking takes place, for instance, when the sender confirms safe receipt of a letter that confirmed safe receipt of a sum of money; the same person carries the letters both ways. This double-checking is justified by the fact that, sometimes, letters get lost along the way.

γινώσκειν σε θέλω ὅτι ἐκομισάμην σου ἐπιστόλιον διὰ Ἑρμείνου τοῦ κοινοῦ φίλου ὡς κομισαμένο[υ σο]υ παρ᾽ αὐτοῦ εἰς τὸν ἐμὸν λόγον ἀρ[ι]θμοῦ (δραχμὰς) μ.

I want you to know that I received your letter through our common friend Herminos, stating that you had received from him 40 *drachmai* to be credited on my account.[125]

---

[120] P.Mich. 8.514.13-14 (III AD); see also PSI 8.900.5-6 (III/IV AD).

[121] SB 16.12322. 5-7 (I AD).

[122] P.Oslo 2.47.8-10 (AD 1).

[123] SPP 22.61.3-6 (II/III AD). For additional references to similar cases in family letters, see Blumell 2014 : 48, n. 74.

[124] P.Mich. 8.499.12-14 (II AD); transl. Blumell 2014 : 49, n. 76.

[125] P.Mert. 1.24.3-6 (ca. AD 200).

ἐ[κ]ọμ̣ειϲ̣ά̣μην ϲου ἐπιϲτόλιον δι' [οὗ] μοι γρ̣[άφ]ει[ϲ] δ̣[ύ]ο ἐπιϲτολάϲ μοι ἀπεϲταλ̣κένẹ. ἴϲθι, ἄ̣δẹλφε, ὅτ̣ι μείαν μόνην ἐκομειϲάμην.

I have received your letter by which you write to me that you sent me two letters. Know, brother, that I received only one.[126]

γεινώϲκιν ϲε θέλω ὅτι τὰϲ ἐπιϲτολὰϲ ἃϲ ἐδήλωϲαϲ διὰ τῆϲ ἐπιϲτολῆϲ καὶ τὸ βιβλίον, ὃ δέδωκαϲ τῷ τοῦ Πατ'τάπε, πάντα ἐκομιϲάμην.

I want you to know that the letters, which you had announced by letter, and the book, which you had given to Pattape's man, I received them all.[127]

καλῶϲ ποιήϲειϲ ϲημάναϲ μοι εἰ παρὰ Νικαγόρου ἢ παρὰ Ἰϲιδώρου κεκόμιϲαι ἢ πυροὺϲ ἢ ἐνέχυρον, εἰ καὶ Διόδωρόϲ ϲοι τὰ γράμματα ἢ οὔ (...).

Please let me know if you have received, either from Nikagoras or from Isidoros, either the wheat or the deposit, and if Diodoros also (brought) you the writing or not (...).[128]

Business letters in a private context were not the only ones to go astray: a *strategos* also acknowledges the loss of some official letters.

καṭαϲṭạθεὶϲ ϲτρ(ατηγὸϲ) ṭ[ῷ] α̣ (ἔτει) μηνὶ Φ̣α̣ῶ̣φ[ι] πρὸϲ πάϲαϲ τὰϲ κομιϲθείϲαϲ μοι ἐπιϲτολὰϲ τυγχάνω ἀντιγρά̣ψ̣αϲ. ἐπεὶ δὲ ϲυμβ[α]ί̣νει παρ' αἰτίαν τῶν διακομιζόντων παραπείπτειν τ[ι]ναϲ, καλῶϲ πο[ι]ήϲειϲ δ̣ηλώϲαϲ μọι εἰ [ἔχ]ειϲ ἐπιϲτολὴν δεομ[έ]νηṿ [τ]ῆϲ ἀπ' ἐμοῦ ἀ[ν]τιφωνήϲεωϲ.

After I was appointed as *strategos* in year 1, in the month of Phaophi, I made copies of all the letters that were entrusted to me. Since, however, it happens that through the messengers' fault some were lost, would you please let me know if you have a letter that lacks a reply from me.[129]

In a family context, a single sheet of papyrus can hold several letters, making it easier for the sender to reach simultaneously more than one member of his family.[130] The sender can

[126] P.Mich. 15.752.29-32 (late II AD).

[127] P.Ross.Georg. 3.4.6-9 (III AD [?]).

[128] PSI 1.95.2-7 (III AD).

[129] P.Oxy. 60.4060.56-59 (AD 161), quoted by Cuvigny 2019 : 81. In P.Lond. 7.2033.2-4 (257-248 BC), letters were eaten by mice; the same happens also in P.Panop. Beatty 1.390-391 (AD 298).

[130] E.g. BGU 2.615 (II AD); P.Oxy. 36.2789 (III AD); also P.Wisc. 2.84 and SB 3.6263 (both AD 175-199), belonging to the Archive of Satornila and her sons; Rowlandson 1998 : 143-144.

also bundle letters together.[131] This presumably corresponds to the ἀπόδεσμοι that appear in the postal service maintained by the army in the Eastern Desert.[132]

> ἔπεμψά σοι τὰ ἐπιστόλια Αἰμιλλιανοῦ καὶ Ῥούφου καὶ Χαρίτωνος.
>
> I have sent you the letters of Aemilianus and Rufus and Chariton.[133]

> συνέδησα ἐπιστọλήν μου καὶ ἄλλην τοῦ ἐνθάδε νομικοῦ πρὸς τὸν παρὰ σοὶ νομικόν.
>
> I have attached my own letter together with another from the local notary, addressed to the notary who is established in your place.[134]

> κόμισον παρὰ Ἡραΐσκο̣[υ] ἐπιστόλια δύο ⟦. .⟧ δε̣δ̣[εμέ]να (...).
>
> Receive from Heraiskos two letters attached (...).[135]

When the sender is forwarding a request from another person, he may send the original written request together with his own letter.

> νομίζω δὲ τ̣ὴν δέησιν αὐτοῦ μὴ εἶναί σοι φορτικ̣ὴν φίλῳ σου ὄντι. ἔπεμψα δέ σοι καὶ `τὰ παρ᾽´ αὐτοῦ γράμματα.
>
> I believe that his request is not a burden to you since he is a friend of yours. Besides, I have sent also the writing I received from him.[136]

4.3 Informant

The bearer of a letter may travel back and forth between the original sender and his correspondent, and can therefore deliver some information.

> δὸς τῷ κομείζοντί σου τὴν ἐπιστολὴν τὴν λαογραφίαν Μνησιθέου καὶ τὸ ναύβιον, καὶ πέμψον ἡμεῖν περὶ τῶν βιβλίον ἧ ἐξήρτισας.
>
> Give Mnesitheos' poll-tax and canal-tax to the person who is bringing this letter to you, and send (a reply) to us about the books, (telling us) how you dispatched them.[137]

---

[131] Incidentally, this provides a possible explanation for the fact that some letters lack an address. It was suggested in P.Oxy. 31.2599 that a letter without an address could have been enclosed in a parcel.

[132] Cuvigny 2019 : 80.

[133] P.Mich. 8.498.20-22 (II AD).

[134] P.Oxy. 41.2983.4-7 (II/III AD).

[135] O.Claud. 2.250.3-5 (II AD).

[136] P.Oslo 2.60.8-11 (II AD).

[137] P.Oxy. 2.296.3-7 (AD 37).

ὁ φέρων σοι τὸ ὄστρακον συνστρέφι .[.] πρὸς ἐμέ. διὰ αὐτοῦ μὴ ἀμελήσῃς γράψαι περὶ τῆς κατ᾽ οἰκίας ἀπογραφῆς.

The person who is carrying this potsherd is returning to me. Take care to write through him about the house census.[138]

Requests for personal information about the recipient's health belong for the most part to the category of family letters.

ἐὰν μὴ ἦν σοι ἀβαρός, ⟦καὶ παρ⟧ γράψον μοι ἐπιστολὴν διὰ τοῦ ἀναδιδόντος σοι τὸ ἐπιστόλιον περεὶ τῆς ὑγίας σου.

If this were not too much trouble for you, write me a letter about your health through the person who is carrying this letter.[139]

The bearer may add some oral information to the content of a letter, or bring some feedback to the sender, either spontaneously or because he has been instructed to do so.[140]

(...) καὶ δήλωσόν μοι διὰ τοῦ κομίζοντός σοι αὐτὴν ὅστις ἐκομίσθη.

(…) and inform me, through the person who is carrying (the letter), who came back.[141]

(...) καὶ ἐ[π]ιγ[νοὺς] τί θέλει ὁ κομίζων {`σοι τὸ <ὑπόμνημα>´}, διο[ρ]θῶσε τὸ ὑπόμνημα

(…) and once you have taken note of what the bearer (of the petition) wants, correct the petition.[142]

The bearer of a letter can also assist in administrative tasks on behalf of the sender. In one case, he brings some documents that require registration by an office, and will then forward them to an archive.

τῷ γὰρ ἀναδιδοῦντί σοι τὸ ἐπιστόλιον ἔδωκα δημοσιώσεις δύο καὶ τούτων τὰς ἐπιστολὰς καὶ (δραχμὰς) λβ· τὸν οὖν τούτων χρηματισμὸν εὐθέως, καθὼς ἔθος ἔχεις, ἀπαρτίσας δώσεις αὐτῷ ἢ ᾧ ἐὰν δοκιμάσῃς ἑτέρῳ ἀσφαλεῖ εἰς τὴν Διδύμου τράπεζαν πρὸς τῇ βιβλιοθή<κῃ> ἢ εἰς τὸ Ἡρακλείδου νομογραφῖον.

To the person who is delivering this letter to you, I have given two documents for registration, together with the letters accompanying them and 32 *drachmai*. So arrange the registration

---

[138] O.Florida 14.13-15 (late II AD).

[139] P.Oxy. 14.1757.17-22 (II AD). PSI 14.1440.5-7 (II/III AD) seems to contain a similar request for a reply to be forwarded through the bearer.

[140] Head 2009 : 289.

[141] P.Flor. 2.255.5-8 (mid-III AD).

[142] BGU 3.829.6-7, corrected from the current text καὶ ἐ[ν]τ[άχιο]ν θέλει ὁ κομίζων `σοι τὸ´ διο[ρ]θῶσε τὸ ὑπόμνημα. This letter is similar to a business letter, but was actually writen by a prefect of Egypt. See Schubert 2018a.

swiftly, as you are used to, then give them to him or to any person you may deem trustworthy at Didymos' bank (for transmission) towards the archive or to Herakleides' notary office.[143]

4.4 Carrier of other items

The bearer of a letter often carries some goods for the recipient. The wording, however, can be misleading because the sender does not specify clearly who is sending the goods, and who is carrying them.

κόμισαι παρὰ Πετεχῶντ(ος) ἀγρίας ἀσταφίδος μ( ) α, ὃν ἐ̣δή̣λω̣σεν Διογᾶς πέπομ[φέναι (...)].

Receive from Petechon one (...) of wild raisins, which Diogas indicated he had sent (...).[144]

It seems that Petechon is the original sender of the goods; we do not know what precise role Diogas played in the transmission. The sender of the letter implies that the raisins are being brought together with the letter, although this is not said explicitly. In this other document, we can suppose that Kephalas is the bearer of the letter.

κόμισαι διὰ Κεφαλᾶτος Πετεχῶ(ντος) Σαλβίου τὴν λαογραφίαν μου (δραχμὰς) ιβ.

Receive through Kephalas son of Petechon, grandson of Salvius, the (amount for) poll tax, 12 *drachmai*.[145]

In the following examples, a clear relation between the wares and the bearer of the letter can be established.

cattle (?)	P.Oxy. 78.5180.2-5 (II/III AD).
food	P.Mich. 3.213.7-14 (III AD).
olives	P.Fay. 130.15-16 (III AD); P.Oxy. 14.1770.14-17 (late III AD).
beans	P.Oxy. 14.1765.25-26 (III AD).
pomegranates	P.Hamb. 1.90.11-13 (mid-III AD); P.Oxy. 14.1757.16-17 (later than AD 138).
honeycomb	P.Laur. 1.20.11-12 (first half III AD).
cheese	P.Laur. 3.102 verso.10-12 (III AD).
bread	P.Mert. 2.85.9-11 (later than AD 229/230).
wheat (in jugs)	SB 5.8002.4-7 (III AD [?]).

[143] P.Oxy. 34.2726.12-28 (II AD).

[144] SB 26.16608.25-29 (= P.Yale 1.77; ca. AD 100).

[145] P.Oxy. 14.1756.4-7 (I AD).

dried fruit and pinecones	BGU 3.801.12-18 (II AD).
palm wine and other jugs	P.Brook. 17.4-9 (III AD).
basket	P.Mich. 8.481.5-8 (early II AD); BGU 2.615.11-13 (II AD); P.Med. 1.74.3-6 (= SB 5.7999; II AD); P.Oxy. 6.936.5-16 (III AD).
bags	P.Oxy. 6.937.29-30 (III AD).
clothing	P.Mert. 3.113.14-19 (II AD).
sandals[146]	P.Oxy. 47.3356 (AD 76); PSI 3.206.8-11 (III AD).
shoe soles	PSI 13.1332.7-9 (= SB 5.7992; II/III AD).
purple dye	P.Oxy. 6.931.4-6 (II AD).
fleece, oil, medical supplies	PSI 8.900.3-5 and 14 (III/IV AD).
books	P.Mil.Vogl. 1.11 (first half II AD).
papyrus	P.Oxy. 14.1765.25-26 (III AD).
parchment	P.Oxy. 17.2156.7-11 (IV/V AD).
seals	P.IFAO 2.40.7-10 (III AD [?]).
money	P.Oxy. 36.2786.3-4 (I AD); BGU 7.1677.3-4 (II AD); P.Oslo 2.54.3-5 (II/III AD); SB 26.16762.7-9 (IV/V AD).
sealed order	P.Oxy. 14.1677.5-7 (III AD).
undefined	P.Oxy. 78.5180.2-4; P.Mil.Vogl. 4.254.4-7 (III AD); SB 6.9549.5-7 (III AD); PSI 3.236.10-15 (III/IV AD).[147]

In one instance, the letter's bearer is carrying a basket with several items, and the recipient should get some other stuff from two different persons.

> κόμισαι παρὰ Σύρου κλουίον ὠ̣ῶν π καὶ βαυκάλιον ὅπ̣ου τριχοίνεικον σινάπεως καὶ ἡμίχουν ἐλαίου ῥαφανίνου καὶ βαυκάλιον ὅπ̣ο̣υ̣ ἡμίχουν μέλιτος καὶ τὸ ξιφίδιν. κόμισαι παρὰ Ἀγαθημέρου μελικηρίδα καὶ κύθραν πλακούντων ι καὶ μελίτινα̣ στεφάνια γ· ταῦτα δῦς τῇ ἀδελφῇ μου καὶ ἀσπάζου αὐτὴν λείαν. κόμισαι παρὰ τοῦ κομίζοντός σοι τὸ ἐπιστόλιον κλουίον ἔχον μ καὶ σφυρίδιον Κανωπικὸν ὅπ̣ου ζεύγη ἄρτων δ καὶ ϛ ζεύγη σκωρσελ̣ε̣ίνας.

> Receive from Syros a basket of 80 eggs and a jug with 3 *choinikes* of mustard and half a *chous* of *raphanos* oil and a jug with half a *chous* of honey and the dagger. From Agathemeros receive a honeycomb and a pot of 10 cakes and 3 honey-sweet garlands; give these to my sister

[146] Sandals are frequently sent together with a letter, see Russo 2004 : 36.

[147] Mutilated text; it seems that the sender is forwarding some money through the bearer of the letter, asking that this money be transmitted to another person.

and salute her warmly. Receive from the bearer of the letter a basket containing 40 eggs (?) and a Canopic basket with 4 pairs of loaves and 6 pairs of (...).[148]

This suggests that several parcels were put together and placed into the hands of one person, together with the letter. The delivery of a basket – with unspecified contents – is also announced by the sender of a letter.

ἐάν σοι ἐνέκῃ καλάθιν ὁ κομιζόμενος σοι τὸ ἐπιστόλειον, πέμ[π]ω.

If the person who is carrying this letter delivers a basket to you, I am sending it.[149]

In the following case, the bearer of the letter is expected to, first, hand money to the recipient of the letter, who is the sender's mother; second, with this money, she will reclaim from a pawnbroker some clothes that belong to her son; and third, the bearer will carry the clothes back to the original sender of the letter.

κόμισ[αι] παρὰ Χ[αιρ]ήμονος τ[ο]ῦ κομίζοντός σο[ι] τὸ [ἐπι]στόλιον ἀργυρίου δραχμὰς ἑκατὸν δέκ[α] δύο, ἐξ ὧν δώσεις Σαραπίωνι τῶι φίλω[ι] τῶι τοῦ Ἀπεὶ λυτρώσασά μου τὰ ἱμάτια δραχμὰς ἑκατὸν καὶ εἰς λ[ό]γον τόκου δραχμὰς ὀκτὼ καὶ σοὶ εἰς δαπάνην τῆς ἱορτῆς δραχμὰς τέσσαρας.

Receive from Chairemon, who is bringing this letter to you, one hundred and twelve *drachmai*, from which you will give to Sarapion, the friend of Apis, to redeem my clothes, one hundred *drachmai*, for the interest eight *drachmai*, and for the expense of the celebration, four *drachmai*.[150]

In another case, the bearer should collect some wine and he brings money to pay for it.

καλ[ῶς] ποιήσις, ἄδελφε, δύο [ἁ]π̣λᾶ μονόχωρα οἴν[ου] διαπεμψάμενός μοι διὰ τοῦ ἀναδιδόντι σο[ι τ]ὰ γράμ(ματα) κομισάμενος παρ' αὐτοῦ εἰς τὴν τι[μ]ὴν αὐτῶν (δραχμὰς) κ.

Please, brother, send two single *monochora* of wine through the person who is delivering this writing to you. You will receive from him 20 *drachmai* for their price.[151]

Judging from the preserved testimonies, the sending of additional items to the recipient happens mostly in family letters – less so in business letters – with the wording κόμισαι παρὰ τοῦ ἀναδιδόντος σοι τὴν ἐπιστολήν 'receive from the person who is delivering this letter to you'. In a family letter that includes business matters, a rather complicated exchange takes place.

[148] P.Oxy. 6.936.5-16 (III AD); transl. Grenfell & Hunt. For another comparable instance, P.Mil.Vogl. 2.70.2-8 (II AD).

[149] BGU 2.615.11-13 (II AD).

[150] P.Oxy. 3.530.10-17 (II AD).

[151] SB 6.9415 (17).3-9 (AD 249-268).

[τῷ ἀναδιδό]ṿτι σοι τὸ ἐπιστόλιον Θη[βα]ί̣[ῳ] δ̣[ὸς] (δραχμὰς) κδ ὀφειλομένας αὐτῷ, κομισ̣αμένη ἀγκάλας ἀμπελίνας α̣ . . (...) κόμισ̣[αι π]αρὰ τοῦ Θηβαίου σάκκον. ὃ̣ν πρ[ό]τρεψα̣ι̣ ταχέως ἐλθεῖν, ἐπ̣εὶ αὐτὸς ἐπὶ τῷ χώματι μ̣έλλε̣[ι] μ̣έ̣ν̣ειν. φησὶ δὲ εἰδέναι κα̣ὶ̣ ἰ̣χ̣θ̣ύας θηρᾶν.

To the Theban who is delivering this letter to you, give 24 *drachmai* that are owed to him; you will receive (...) vine bundles. (...) Receive from the Theban one bag. You should push him to come quickly, because he himself intends to stay on the dike. He claims he also knows how to catch fish.[152]

In the following example, the bearer of the letter is not presented explicitly as such, but the various roles ascribed to Didymos, who appears in the letter, leave little room for a doubt that he is indeed carrying the message, together with some goods; and he must bring back some information.

διεπεμψάμη[ν σ]οι διὰ Διδύμου δέρματα βότια τὸν δὲ ἀριθμὸν αὐτῳ μεταδώσι σοι ὁ αὐτὸς Δίδυμος καὶ ψιάθους ἐμοῦ μόνου μεμιλτομένας λη, κ[ο]ινωνιμέας μεθ' Ἡρακλείδου πβ ὧν τὸ ἥ`μ´ισύ ἐστιν ἐμοῦ, τῆς δαπάνης πάσης τῶν τε βοτίων καὶ πασῶν τῶν ψιάθων οὔσης πρὸς Ἡρακλείδην. τὰ ἀργύρια ἐὰν συνλέξῃς εὐθέως διὰ ἐπιθήκης διαπέμψαι μοι. δήλοσόν μοι πόσα βότια παρέλεβης καὶ πόσης τιμῆς πιπράσκετε, καὶ πόσαι ψίαθοι ἀποκειται ἀπὸ τοῦ προτέρου φορτίου, καὶ σὺν τούτοις πόσαι ἀπόκεινται. ταῦτα δὲ πάντα διὰ τοῦ αὐτοῦ Διδύμου δηλώσις μοι. εὐθέως δὲ τὸν αὐτὸν Δίδυμον ἀπόλυσον, ἵνα μὴ ἐπὶ πλῖον παρέλκηται παρὰ σοί.

I have sent you through Didymos some sheepskins – the same Didymos will let you know how many of them there are – and some mats, of which thirty-eight, dyed red, belong to me alone, eighty-one I own together with Herakleides; half of these are mine, but all the expense for the sheepskins and for all the mats is for Herakleides to pay. If you collect the money, send it to me at once by letter of credit. Tell me how many sheepskins you received and at what price they are selling, and how many mats are in stock from the last shipment and how many are in stock counting these. You are to let me know all this through the same Didymos. Let the same Didymos go at once, so that he may not be detained longer with you (...).[153]

Also in two family letters, control devices appear; they allow the senders to ensure that goods accompanying the letter do not disappear along the way.

κόμισον οὖν [. . . .] παρὰ τοῦ ἀναδιδουντι τ̣[αῦ]τά μου τὰ γράμματα ἀγ'γε̣ῖ̣ο̣ν̣ ἐλέου καὶ δὸς αὐτὸ Ἱέρακει, ἔχων ἐπιγραφὴν Ὡρίων φ (...).

Receive therefore (…) from the person who is delivering this writing of mine a jar of oil and give it to Hierax – it has the inscription 'Horion' (φ) (...).[154]

[152] P.Oxy. 59.3990.3-6 and 16-20 (II AD).

[153] P.Oxy. 49.3505.3-19 (II AD [?]; transl. A. Bülow-Jacobsen). For a similar situation, see also P.Oxy. 31.2596.3-9 (III AD).

[154] P.Oxy. 14.1770.14-19.

κόμισε διὰ τοῦ ἀναδι[δόντος σ]οι τὸ ἐπι[σ]τόλιον Πωλίωνος [κεράμ]ια ἐσφ[ρ]αγισμένα β ὀ̣λ̣ύ[ρας σφρ]α̣γῖδα ἔχουσα γλύμματι [Σαχ]ύ[ψ]εως Καλοῦς Μεγιστοῦς.

Receive through Polion, who is delivering this letter to you, 2 jars of wheat with a seal depicting Sachypsis Kalos Megistos.[155]

To sum up, the delivery and the collection of items does not seem to be symmetrical: the former is far better represented in family letters, whereas the latter appears most frequently in business letters, as we shall see below.

4.5 Recipient of other items

In most instances, the bearer of a business letter is not bringing any goods to the recipient, but on the contrary has come to collect something.

water	O.Krok. 1.78.4-6 (ca. AD 98-117).
wine	O.Stras. 1.792.3-5 (I BC – I AD); P.Flor. 2.274.3-9 (AD 265); P.Prag. 1.111.2-7 (AD 249-269); P.Vind.Sijp. 26.12-14 (late III AD); O.Kellis 140.2-5 (III/IV AD); SPP 8.968.3-5 (IV AD).
acacia juice and incense	P.Ryl. 2.242.5-8 (III AD).
mustard (28 *artabai*!)	P.Fay. 122.3-6 (ca. AD 100).
olives	SB 20.14242.15-16 (I AD).
oil	P.Fouad 1.79.6-10 (III/IV AD).
rose oil	O.Claud. 1.171.4-10 (ca. AD 100-120).
wool	P.Mil.Vogl. 3.201.4-10 (= SB 6.9160; II AD).
hair	P.Vind.Worp 12.7-10 (early I AD).
cloak and coat	PSI 8.900.58 (III/IV AD).
geese	PSI 3.236.34.35 (III/IV AD).
dried fish	SB 24.15946.2-5 (I-IV AD).
wheat	P.Mil.Vogl. 2.59.3-7 (II AD); P.Poethke 14.4-8 (II AD); P.Tebt.Quen. 22 (II/III AD).
barley (300 *artabai*!)	P.Mil.Vogl. 4.257.3-5 (AD 175).
straw	SB 8.9914.3-5 (ca. AD 267).
fodder	P.Ryl. 2.240.3-5 (mid-III AD).

[155] SB 5.8002.4-8 (III AD [?]). On the interpretation of this seal, see Visser 1935 : 269. The label on the seal is grammatically faulty.

waterskin	O.Did. 361.2-4 (AD 76/77).
pruning-knives	P.Brook. 75.2-6 (II AD).
key and tool	BGU 3.775.9-12 (III AD).
medical supplies	P.Oslo 2.54.5-9 (II/III AD).
book	SB 3.7268.12-13 (AD 98-117).
written order	P.Ryl. 2.241.1-7 (III AD).
money	O.Claud. 1.145.4-11 (ca. AD 100-120); P.Oxy. 3.532.10-13 (II AD); P.Oxy. 59.3990.3-5 (II AD); P.Gen. 1^2.2.2-4 (II/III AD); P.Oxy. 14.1773.16-20 (III AD); P.Coll.Youtie 2.88.14-17 (IV AD); SB 24.16336.3-8 (= P.Harr. 1.110; IV AD); P.Herm. 13.3-7 (IV AD).
money (allowance for two months) and coat	P.Oxy. 10.1295.13-16 (= Sel. Pap. 1.129; II/III AD).
false coinage	P.Michael. 12.2-4 (I/II AD).

The amounts to be handed to the bearer can be quite significant, e.g. 28 *artabai* of mustard or 300 *artabai* of barley. Wine and money are the two commodities most often collected from the letter's recipient.

The letter thus functions as an order for delivery or payment; the imperative παράσχες or παράσχου 'provide' sometimes appears in small notes, first in the third century and then more frequently in the fourth.

> τῷ ἀναδιδοῦντί σοι ταῦτά μου τὰ [γ]ράμματα ⟦πρạịι⟧ παράσχες χọ́[ρ]τον.
>
> To the person who is delivering this writing of mine to you, provide some fodder.[156]

> παράσχο\`υ´ [τῷ] ἀναδιδοῦντι σοι τὸ πιττάκιον ὑπὲρ τιμ(ῆς) νο(μισματίων) β οἴνου διπλᾶ ὀγδοήκοντα ὀκτώ.
>
> Provide, to the person who is delivering this ticket to you, eighty double measures of wine to the value of 2 *solidi*.[157]

One item that the bearer of a message must collect remains shrouded in mystery. The recipient is asked to provide the sender's παρτικλάριον.[158] This is clearly a transliteration of the Latin *particularium*, a word without attested parallels, diminutive of *particula*.[159]

[156] P.Ryl. 2.240.3-5 (mid-III AD).

[157] SPP 8.968.3-5 (IV AD).

[158] SPP 22.61.3-4 (II/III AD).

[159] Daris 1991 : 86.

From the context, where the sender specifies that this item should be sent under seal, one can surmise that it is a document, perhaps related to a soldier's status.

4.6 Money transfer

In the catalogue provided in the preceding section, money is the commodity most often collected by the bearer. Letters allow the virtual transfer of money, where a payment made to the bearer balances the accounts in relation with a previous transaction.

> καλῶς πυήσις τοῖς ἀναδιδοῦντι συ ταῦτά μου τὰ γράμματα δοῦνẹ κενοῦ νομίσματος τάλαντα δ[ύ]ọ ἥμισου, γί(ν.) (τάλ.) β̣ (δρ.) Γ, ἀ̣[νθ' ὧν αἰτήσα]σα̣ ἔσσχον ἀπ' αὐτῶ[ν ἐν τῷ Τυ]ραννίῳ εἰς λόγον φ[ορέτρο]υ.
>
> Please give to those who deliver to you this letter of mine two and a half *talanta* of new coinage, that is, 2 *tal.* 3000 *dr.*, in return for that which I asked for and got from them in the Tyrannion on account of transportation charges (…).[160]

> καὶ ἔσχο(ν) παρ' αὐτοῦ (δραχμὰς) η, ἵν<α> δώσεις αὐτῷ τ̣ὰ̣ς ἴσας.
>
> And I received from him 8 *drachmai*, so that you should give him the same amount.[161]

> [εὐθ]έ̣ως δεξάμενός μου τὰ γράμματα ἐξο̣δ̣ίᾳ̣σον τῷ ἀ̣δ̣ε̣λ̣φῷ Ἰσιδώρῳ τῷ καὶ ἀναδιδόντι σοι ταῦτά̣ μ̣ο̣υ τὰ γράμματα ἀργυρίου Σεβαστῶν [ν]ο̣μίσμ̣ατος τάλαντα ἑξήκοντα τρία, γ̣ί̣ν̣(ονται) (τάλαντα) ξγ, ἀνθ' ὧν ἔσχον παρ' αὐτοῦ ἐν[θάδε ἐν] Ἡρακλέους εἰς λόγον τιμῆς.
>
> As soon as you receive this writing of mine, pay in full to my brother Isidoros, who is also delivering to you this writing of mine, sixty-three *talanta* of imperial silver (= 63 *tal.*), for which I received from him here in town, for this price (…).[162]

> καλῶς οὖν ποιήσεις μεταβαλόμενος Ἀλεξάνδρῳ τῷ διδόντι σοι τὴν ἐπιστολὴν, ἀφ' οὗ τὰς ἴσας ἤδη ἔσχον.
>
> Please pay over (the price of the pig) to Alexandros, who is giving you this letter, from whom I have already received the same amount.[163]

Thus, instead of forwarding money in cash, the sender makes a payment order, producing – as it were – a cheque to the bearer.

---

[160] P.Oxy. 14.1773.16-22 (III AD); transl. Bagnall & Cribiore 2006 : 371.

[161] SB 5.8002.9-10 (III AD [?]); see also O.Claud. 2.266 and P.Gen. 1^2.2, quoted above.

[162] SB 26.16482.2-7 (late III / early IV AD).

[163] P.Oxy. 42.3085.6-10 (III AD).

4.7 Escort

The bearer can be sent to fetch someone who is involved in a family or business relationship with the sender. In such cases, the bearer assumes no police duty, but is nonetheless entrusted with some authority on behalf of the sender.

> διὸ παρακαλῶ σε εὐθέως λαβών μου τὰ γράμματα παρὰ Σαραπάμμωνος ἐξελθῖν σὺν αὐτῷ εἰς δι . . . .[.] . ε. κἀγὼ ἐν τῇ ἀνάγκῃ σο[υ οὐ π]ạρεῖδόν σε καὶ διότι κἀγὼ [ἐν τῇ φ]ịλạνθρωπίạ μου παρά σοι ἐ[ξῆλθον.
>
> Therefore I beseech you, as soon as you receive this writing of mine from Sarapammon, set off with him to (...). I too, when you were in need, did not neglect you, and for this reason I too, in my kindness, set off to see you.[164]

> ἐὰν ᾖ σοι ἀβαρές, σκυλεὶς πρὸς Θέονα τὸν σκυτέα καὶ Γερόντιον ποίησον αὐτοὺς γενέσθαι πρὸς μὲ ἅμα τῷ τ̣ὰ [γρ]ά̣μ̣ματά σοι ἐπιφέροντι, καὶ Διοσκουρίδην δὲ τὸν χρυσοχόον.
>
> If this is not too much of a burden for you, hurry to Theon the cobbler and to Gerontios, and make them come to me together with the person who is carrying this writing to you, and also Diskourides the goldsmith.[165]

> [πέμ]ψεις μου τὴν ἀδελφὴν [διὰ τ]ọῦ ἀναδ̣ιδομένου σοι ταῦ[τα τ]ạ̀ γράμματά μου.
>
> You shall send my sister through the person who is delivering to you this writing of mine.[166]

4.8 Police duties

Strictly speaking, warrants are not letters, or at least their format partially differs from that of a business letter.[167] For most practical purposes, however, they function in a similar fashion. In warrants, the explicit mention of the bearer with a wording such as παράδοτε τῷ ἀποσταλέντι ὑπ' ἐμοῦ στρατιώτῃ 'deliver to the soldier whom I have sent', indicates that the soldier carrying the warrant is entrusted with some kind of police authority that allows him to seize the wanted person. It seems virtually certain that he is also the bearer of the warrant.

Ursula Hagedorn noticed that, in the mid-third century, the format of warrants undergoes a change, presumably linked to the administrative reform introduced by emperor Philip the

---

164 SB 14.12026.5-12 (II/III AD).

165 P.Oxy. 34.2727.18-24 (III/IV AD).

166 P.Flor. 3.365.10-12 (III AD [?]).

167 On warrants (also called 'orders for arrest' or 'summonses'), see esp. G.M. Browne in his introduction to P.Mich. 10.589-591; most recently P.Cair.Preis.^{2} 5 and BGU 20.2861; Drexhage 1989; Gagos & Sijpesteijn 1996; Schubert 2018b.

Arab.[168] For a period of a few decades between the late third and early fourth centuries, warrants carry an explicit mention of the man who is obviously the bearer: he is sent forth to bring a person in the presence of the official who has issued the warrant. Before and after this short interval, the recipient is responsible for escorting the individual; or else, we should assume that the bearer's mission is implicitly stated, which seems implausible, given the clear chronological boundary between both types of warrants. The wording used to describe the dispatch of the wanted person is also not the same in the two periods. In the first example quoted below (II/III AD), the bearer does not appear, and the verb used for the dispatch is ἀναπέμψετε 'send over'; in the second example (III/IV AD), a soldier has been sent, he is presumably carrying the warrant, and the order is expressed with the verb παράδοτε 'hand over'.

> ἀρχεφόδοις καὶ τοπάρχῃ κώμης Σοκνοπαίου Νήσου̣. ἀ̣ναπ̣έ̣μψαται Ἀβοῦν γέρδιν̣ καὶ Καιεῦν γέρδιν καὶ γυναῖκα Ἀβοῦτός ποτε τοπάρχου γερδίαιναν καὶ ταύτης θυγατέραν οὖσαν γερδίαιναν, ἐνκαλουμένους ὑπὸ Ἀμμωνίου, ἐξαυτῆς.
>
> To the chiefs of police and to the local chief of the village of Soknopaiou Nesos. Send over Abous and the wife of Abous, formerly local chief, and her daughter, all three weavers, who are being accused by Ammonios, immediately.[169]

> ἀρχεφόδοις καὶ δημοσίοις κώμης Φιλαδελφίας. ἐξαυτῆς παράδοτε τῷ ἀποσταλέντι ὑπ' ἐμοῦ στρατιώτῃ Νόννον καὶ Ἰούλιον καὶ Πεσοῦριν Χρυσᾶ καὶ Πέκυσιν Ἐπαγαθοῦ καὶ Πλανητὴν καὶ Ἀμμώνιον ἐνκαλουμένους ὑπὸ τ̣ῶν ἀπὸ τῆς κώμης ἢ ὑμεῖς αὐτοὶ ἥκετε.
>
> To the chiefs of police and officials of the village of Philadelphia. Hand over immediately, to the soldier whom I sent, Nonnus, Iulius and Pesouris sons of Chrysas, Pekysis son of Epagathos, Planetes and Ammonios, who are accused by the villagers; or else come yourselves.[170]

This phenomenon occurs also in an *ostrakon* that was – hesitantly – dated to the second century AD. The dating, however, is not secure enough to reject Hagedorn's limitation to the late third and early fourth centuries.

---

[168] Hagedorn 1979 : 73. On the administrative reform, P.Oxy. 61.4114-4116 (p. 91); Parsons 1967; Bianchi 1983.

[169] BGU 11.2083.1-4 (II/III AD).

[170] P.Wisc. 1.24.2-5 (dated to II/III AD in the *editio princeps*; date corrected to III/IV AD by Hagedorn 1979 : 66).

Ψενμώνθης ἀρχιφύλ(ακι) Ἰβίωνος· παράδος τῷ διδόντι σοι τὸ ὄστρακον Παμώνθην Σενπασή(μιος).

Psenmonthes to the chief of police of Ibion. Hand over Pamonthes son of Senpasemis to the person who delivers this potsherd to you.[171]

In a similar way, a person sent on a police mission may require an escort. In the following case, the structure of the document is not that of a proper letter, but of a business note ordering the delivery of some goods. It was sent by the *strategos* of the Prosopite nome to the village chiefs (κωμάρχαι) and the chief of police (ἀρχέφοδος) of a village. Most probably the guard and donkeys should assist the bearer in bringing someone back to the *strategos*.

π(αρὰ) τοῦ στρατηγοῦ κωμάρχ(αις) καὶ ἀρχεφόδ(ῳ) κώμη(ς) Θερήσεως. δύο ὄνους καὶ ἕνα φύλακα τῷ ἀναδιδοῦντι ὑμεῖν τὰ γράμματα παράσχεται (l. -τε) μέχρι τῆς Μέμφεως.

From the *strategos* to the village chiefs and chief of police of the village of Theresis. Provide two donkeys and one guard to the person who is delivering this writing to you, (accompanying him) till Memphis.[172]

4.9 Recommendation

4.9.1 Introduction and welcome

The bearer of a letter often comes with a request for help addressed to the recipient. This help should benefit either the sender or the bearer himself; in the latter case, the letter serves the purpose of an introduction or recommendation.[173] The sender does not always specify if the recommended person is carrying the letter, or if the message has followed a separate channel of communication.[174]

In the context reminder of the letter, there is frequently a mention of the bearer in the nominative, followed by ἔστι or τυγχάνει ὤν 'he happens to be'.

ὁ ἀν[α]διδούς σοι ταῦτά μου τὰ γράμματα βοηθός ἐστιν τῆς Αἰδιναρίας.

The person who is delivering this writing of mine is Haidinaria's assistant (…).[175]

---

[171] O.Bodl. 2.1992.

[172] P.Oxy. 31.2577.1-6 (mid-III AD); on the provenance of this papyrus, Hagedorn 2001 : 151.

[173] Keyes 1935; Kim 1972.

[174] P.Oxy. 38.2844 (second half I AD), a private letter on a business matter, on behalf of a woman.

[175] P.Stras. 4.172.2-3 (early IV AD).

> [ὁ] ἀναδιδούς σοι τὰ γράμ[ματά] μου οἰκῖος τοῦ πατρὸς [τοῦ Σ]τεφάνου τυγχάνει.
>
> The person who is delivering this writing of mine happens to be a relative of Stephanos' father.[176]

In the two preceding examples, the relation between the letter's sender and bearer is indicated by the words βοηθός 'assistant' and οἰκεῖος 'relative'; in other instances, the bearer is described as φίλος 'friend'.[177] He can also be called υἱός 'son', even though the context indicates that the bearer's father is already dead (see below).[178] A relationship with a third person can be mentioned.

> τὸν ἐπιδίδοντά σοι \`τὴν´ ἐπιστολὴν ὡς ἕνα ἡμῶν ἰδέ. ἔστιν γὰρ Εὐνοΐῳ σύντροφος.
>
> Consider the person who is delivering this letter to you as one of us; for he is close to Eunoios.[179]

More extravagant wording also occurs.

> (...) Θέωνα τὸν παράδοξον τὸν ἀναδιδόντα σοι ταῦτά μου τὰ γράμματα οἰκεῖόν μου ὄντα καὶ σχέσιν ἀδελφικὴν ἔχοντα πρός με.
>
> (...) the extraordinary Theon, who is delivering to you this letter of mine and is a relative of mine and enjoys the status of a brother towards me.[180]

> (...) ἐπιστέλλω σοι ὑπὲρ Διογένου[ς] ̣εω ̣ο̣ς, ἀδελφιδοῦ ὄντος [ἀνα]γκ̣αιοτάτου μοι φίλου, ἀνδρὸς φιλοσόφου γενομένου̣ τ̣ὰ Ἐπικούρια (...).
>
> (...) I am writing to you on behalf of Diogenes son of (...), the nephew of a very close friend of mine, who was a philosopher versed in Epicurean matters (...).[181]

The recommendation can be short and quite vague, as when the sender does not specify what ought to be done but merely asks the recipient to make a deal with the bearer εἰδὼς ὅτι ἐμοὶ διαφέρει 'because you know that this matters to me'.[182] In a letter sent to a *strategos* presumably from a colleague who calls him ἀδελφός 'brother', the request also lacks detail:

---

176 P.Princ. 2.101.7-9 (IV AD).

177 P.Lugd.Bat. 25.31.4-7 (I/II AD); P.Oxy. 20.2275.6 (III/IV AD).

178 P.Oxy. 9.1219.3 (III AD).

179 P.Oxy. 55.3812.12-13 (late III AD).

180 P.Oslo 2.55.3-7 (II/III AD).

181 P.Oxy. 51.3643.5-10.

182 P.Tebt. 2.448.2 (II/III AD).

ἐν οἷς ἐ̣ά̣ν̣ σου δέηται σπουδάσα̣ι̣ α̣ὐ̣τῶι 'to give your care to him in whatever he asks you'.[183] The sender of another letter gives the following justification.

> Σωτῆρα δ̣έ, ἐξ οὗ τ̣[ὴ]ν̣ ἀφορμὴν ἔσχον ἐπιστεῖλαί σ̣[ο]ι, παρατίθε̣μαί σοι, ἄδελφε, ἵνα ὁρᾳ̣ς̣ αὐτὸν ὡς Σερῆνον τ[ὸ]ν μεικρὸν ἡμῶν ἀδελφόν, οὐ μόνον διὰ τὸ ἦθος τὸ χρηστὸν ἄξιον το̣ῦ̣ τυχεῖν ἀλλὰ κ[αί (...).
>
> Since I had an opportunity to send you a letter, I am putting Soter in your charge, so that you may look after him in the same way as our little brother Serenus: he deserves it not only because of his excellent character, but also (...).[184]

The bearer may need some assistance in completing a negotiation where the help of an official is necessary.

> Θέων ὁ υἱὸς ἡμῶν παραγείνεται πρὸς σὲ πορευόμενος εἰς τὴν Νεικίου ἕνεκα ἀναγκαίου αὐτοῦ μετεώρου ἴσως ὃ καὶ σὺ ἐπίστασαι ἔτι πάλαι ἀπὸ τοῦ πατρὸς αὐτοῦ· περιὼν (l. περιόντα) δὲ νομίζω γεγραφέναι σοι περὶ αὐτοῦ. (...) ἀλλὰ οἶδα ὅτι καὶ ταῦτά μου τὰ γράμματα πόλλ' αὐτὸν ὠφελήσει, εἴ τινος [ο]ὗ̣ ἐὰν χρείαν ἔχ̣ῃ εἴτε πρὸς Ἀπ[ί]ωνα τὸν τοῦ Προσωπείτου βασιλικὸν εἴτε πρὸς ἕτερόν τινα, ἐὰν δ̣εή[σῃ] καὶ αὐτοῖς γράψαι μὴ ὑπερθῇ. (verso) Ἀπίωνι υἱῶι βασιλικ(ῷ) γρ(αμματεῖ) Λητοπολ(ίτου) π(αρὰ) Ἀριστάν̣δ̣(ρου) Ὀξ(υρυγχίτου).
>
> Theon our son is coming to you on his way to Nikias' house on account of a pressing incompleted negotiation of which you have perhaps been aware long since from his father; I think that he wrote to you about it while he was still alive. (...) But I know that this letter of mine also will be of much help to him, if he wants anything either from Apion the royal secretary of the Prosopite nome or from any one else, if you will ask them and not delay to write to them. (...). (Address on the back) To my son Apion, royal secretary of the Letopolite nome, from Aristandros of Oxyrhynchos.[185]

Elsewhere, the recipient is asked to help because a superintendant has restrained the letter's bearer and does not want to deal with him.

> σ<ο>ῦ ἀλύπου ὄντος [ὑ]π̣ὸ̣ αὐτοῦ, εἶπέ μοι γὰρ ὅτι εἴ τι βούλεται διδῶ αὐτῷ, καὶ διὰ τοῦτο ἔγραψά σοι. ἐὰν γὰρ σὺ θελήσῃς, γείνεται αὐτοῦ τὸ ἔργον.
>
> You should suffer no damage from him, for he said to me: 'If he wants anything, I give it to him.' And for this reason I wrote to you. For if you wish so, his affair is concluded.[186]

---

[183] P.Giss. 1.71.5-6 (= P.Giss.Apoll. 37, later than AD 117). The same wording appears in another document of the same archive, P.Giss. 1.88.5-6 (= P.Giss.Apoll. 41, AD 113-120).

[184] P.Oxy. 14.1663.6-12 (II/III AD). Although Serenus is not explicitly described as the bearer of the letter, the context makes it quite clear that he is indeed carrying the recommendation.

[185] P.Oxy. 9.1219.3-21 (III AD; transl. A.S. Hunt).

[186] P.Mich. 8.515.3-5 (late III AD).

The bearer does not act on the sender's behalf, but needs an introduction in order to conduct his own business. The superintendant's behaviour, as well as the bearer's alleged claim that he can provide whatever is asked of him, rather suggests that the bearer's reputation has been compromised. Without the sender's recommendation, he presumably has no chance of concluding his affair.

Recommendation letters may be very short and serve only the purpose of introducing or protecting a person; in other cases, as we shall see below, the aim of the letter can be more complex.

4.9.2 Preceding the sender

In many instances, the bearer acts as a substitute for the sender. Such is the function of most business letters, and such was the way people understood letters at the time. The bearer can also be dispatched to prepare the way for the sender.

> Ἡρᾶς ὁ κομίζων σοι τὴν ἐπιστολὴν ἐστὶν γραμματεὺς γεωργῶν ἐν Σκαν[διψ] καὶ ἔχει ⟦συν⟧ ἀπολο[γί]αν δῶναι ὑπὲρ [τῆς ἐπι]δοθείσης ἀναφορᾶς. [πα]ρακαλῶ [σε ἀκολου]θεῖν αὐτῶι πρὸς Μάρκον ἵνα π[ροσδέχηται] αὐτὸν μέχρει παραγένωμαι.
>
> Heras, who is bringing this letter to you, is a farmers' secretary in Skandips and he has an apology to deliver for the delayed report. I ask you to accompany him to Marcus so that (Marcus) can receive him till my arrival.[187]

In the following example, Ammonios, the accompanying person, is not specifically mentioned as the bearer of the letter, but the various tasks he undertakes strongly suggest that he is indeed carrying the message.

> σκύληθι σὺν Ἀμμωνίῳ πρὸς τὸν στρατηγὸν ἵν' αὐτῷ μεταδῷς ἐφ' ὃ παραγείνομαι. ἐπίτηδες γὰρ ἔπεμψα τὸν Ἀμμώνιον. λήμψῃ παρὰ Ἀμμωνίου (δραχμὰς) μη εἰς συνωνὴν χρωματίνων ἐρίων καλαίνων ἐάνπερ λάβῃ παρὰ Λαμυρίου, ἐὰν δ' ἄρα μή, σὺ αὐτὸς προχρήσεις. (...) λήμψῃ παρὰ Ἀμμωνίου φοινει . . . . δύο.
>
> Hurry with Ammonios to the *strategos* so that you may inform him of the purpose of my visit; for this is the reason why I sent Ammonios. You will receive from Ammonios 48 *drachmai* for the purchase of wool coloured in blue-green, provided that you can get some from Lamyrios; or else, you shall borrow some yourself. You will receive from Ammonios two (...).[188]

4.9.3 Advice

The bearer may carry a request for advice; the sender thus acts as a go-between, providing the bearer with access to the recipient. In one such instance, the bearer of the letter wishes to appeal to a *strategos* and needs some advice from the sender's father.

---

[187] P.Oslo 2.51.3-8 (II AD).

[188] P.Haun. 2.22.4-9 and 13-14 (II/III AD).

> Γαλάτου τοῦ κομίζοντός σοι τὸ ἐπιστόλιον μέλλοντος ἐ̣ν̣τυ̣[γχάνειν] τῷ στρα[τ]ηγῷ̣ [. . . . .]ν̣ δι̣ .[. . . .] .α̣υ̣[. . . . .]ν ἡγησ̣ά̣μην̣ διαπέμψασθαι αὐτὸν πρὸ̣ς σὲ ὅπως γνώμη[ν] σου λάβῃ πρότερον περὶ τοῦ πράγματος.
>
> Because Galates, who is bringing this letter to you, is going to meet the *strategos* … I thought to send him to you, so that beforehand he should receive your opinion concerning the matter.[189]

Beyond mere advice, the sender probably expects his father to introduce the bearer to the *strategos* himself.

4.9.4 Purchase

The bearer of a letter may be expected to make a purchase, together with the recipient, on behalf of the sender.

> καλῶς ποιήσεις συνελθὼν [Α]ἰ̣λου̣ρί̣ω̣ν̣ι̣ τῶι κομίζοντί σοι τὸ ἐπ[ι]στ[ό]λιον, ὅπως εἰς τὴν ἑωρτὴν περιστερείδια ἡμεῖν ἀγοράσηι.
>
> Please accompany Ailourion, who is carrying this letter to you, so that you may purchase for us some doves for the party.[190]

> [καλῶς ποι]ήσις, κύριε, π̣ε̣ρ̣ὶ [πο]λ̣λοῦ σοι γενέσθαι Πα[σίωνι τῷ ἀ]ναδιδοῦντί σοι ταῦτά μου τὰ γράμματα [. . . . .] . φίλῳ ἡμῶν συνωνήσασθαι [. . . . ταπ]ή̣τια κάλλιστα ἀφ’ ὧν οἶδες ὅτι κάλλι[στα ἔχουσιν.]
>
> Please, my lord, make your best effort on behalf of Pasion, a friend of ours, who is delivering to you this writing of mine (…), to assist him in buying (…) the most beautiful carpets from those of whom you know that they have the very best.[191]

> τὸν ἀποδιδ[όν]τα ὑμῖν τὸ ἐπιστόλιόν μου [ἀγο]ράζοντα ὀθόνια συνίστημι [ὑμῖν] ἵν’ αὐτῶι σ̣υ̣ν̣έ̣λθητ̣ε ἕ[ως αὐ]τ̣ὰ ἀγοράσῃ̣.
>
> The person who is delivering to you this letter of mine is buying some linen. I put him in your care, asking you to accompany him till he has made his purchase.[192]

There seems to be a kind of universality in such proceedings, which find a striking parallel in Palladius' history of Egyptian monachism, written in the early fifth century.

---

[189] See Blumell 2011 : 36, publication of P.WaPS.05 (Washington State University Collection), lines 3-11 (transl. Blumell).

[190] BGU 2.596.4-8 (AD 84). In P.Lugd.Bat. 25.31 (I/II AD), the nature of the intended purchase is lost.

[191] P.Oxy. 20.2275 (III/IV AD).

[192] P.Stras. 4.174.3-6 (II/III AD). The reading ἵν’ αὐτῶι σ[υ]ν[π]άθητε, provided in the *editio princeps*, seems awkward. Paul Heilporn (Strasbourg) kindly provided me with an image of the papyrus, where the reading σ̣υ̣ν̣έ̣λ|θητ̣ε seems preferable.

> ἐν οἷς καὶ ὁ καλὸς Ἀφθόνιος ὁ φίλος μου γενόμενος γνήσιος, τὸ νῦν δευτερεύων ἐν τῷ μοναστηρίῳ· ὃν ὡς ἀσκανδάλιστον ἀποστέλλουσιν ἐν Ἀλεξανδρείᾳ ἐπὶ τὸ διαπωλῆσαι μὲν αὐτῶν τὰ ἔργα, συνωνήσασθαι δὲ τὰς χρείας.
>
> Among them is also the endearing Aphthonios, who was my genuine friend and is presently the second in command in the monastery. With his impeccable credentials, they are sending him to sell their production in Alexandria, and to help in the purchase of the necessary goods.[193]

The bearer can also be sent to collect a whole shipping of goods. The following example, which is quite straightforward in its wording, consists of only the three basic structural elements of a business letter, i.e. heading, required action, and closing greetings, together with a mention of the bearer. The required action is described in detail and takes most of the space in the letter.

> τοῦ ἀναδιδόντος σοι τὸ ἐπιστόλιόν μου ναυκλήρου Πανẹμοụῶτος προνόησον σὺν (?) πάσῃ σπουδῇ ἐνβαλέσθαι αὐτοῦ τὸν γόμον ὡς ἔθọς ọ̔ν [ἔ]χεις ἐν χερσὶ καὶ λ̣εκτῷ ἐνβαλέσθαι, καὶ τοὺς δειγματοάρτας καθ' αὐτὸν ἀναπέμψαι πρὸς ζυγοστα[σ]ίαν λαβόντα παρὰ τῶν ἀρχεφόδων ὀνάριον. ἀπεντεῦθεν μὲν ο̣[ὖ̂ν] συνσκυλῆθ̣ι̣ αὐτῷ καὶ ἰδέτω τοὺς θησαυρούς, κα[ὶ] τοὺς [σι]τολόγους καὶ τοὺς ἄλλους τοὺς πρὸς τὴ̂ν χρείαν ὧ̂ν τὰ ὀνόματά σοι ἔπεμψεν Ἁρποκρατίων ἐν ἑτοίμῳ ποίησον ἵνα μη[δ]ὲν ἐνπόδιον ἦ̂ν.
>
> The bearer of this letter is the captain Panemouos; see to it with all your care to embark his freight, as usual what you have in hand and have selected for lading. Send up the inspectors yourself to the examination, getting a donkey from the chiefs of police. After this give him your best attention and let him see the granaries, and prepare the grain collectors and the other officials concerned, whose names have sent to you by Harpocration, in order that there may be no delay.[194]

The sender thoroughly describes the assistance needed from the recipient so that the bearer can perform the prescribed task. One element may explain the absence of any exhortation or justification: the letter is addressed to the sender's assistant (verso: Ἀρχελάωι ὑπηρέτῃ). The hierarchical relation between the two makes any further argument unnecessary.

4.9.5 Escort and protection from hassle

The bearer of a letter may need protection along the way, especially if he is carrying some valuable items. The context of the following letter strongly suggests that the goods are in the same hands as the bearer of the letter.

[193] Pallad. *Hist. Laus.* 32.8.

[194] P.Oxy. 1.63.3-18 (II/III AD; transl. adapted from Grenfell & Hunt).

> ἔπεμψα Ἔρωτα τὸν ἡμέτε[ρο]ν. διὸ ἐρωτῶ συνλαβοῦ αὐτῷ ὅπως διὰ σο[ῦ εἰ]ς οἶκον διασωθῇ. ἔδωκα γὰρ αὐτῷ εἰς ἀνακομιδὴν δι[̣] ̣ ̣ ̣ κε. ẹ̣ἀ̣ν σοι εὔκαιρον ᾖν παρ̣ά̣π̣[εμψον ἀ]ν̣ακομίζοντα αὐτọ̀ν.
>
> I have sent Eros, our man (slave?). Therefore I ask you to assist him so that, with your help, he may reach home safely. For I have given him for delivery 25 (...). If you find an opportunity, send someone to escort him for the delivery.[195]

A letter of recommendation may also facilitate the transfer of a body from the Arsinoite nome downstream to Alexandria.

> ἀξιώσω οὖν, κύρ<ι>ε μου, εἵνα δῷς αὐτοῖς γράμματα εἵνα μηδὶς ἐνοχλήσι αὐτοῖς καθ' ὁδόν, εἵνα δυνηθῶ κηδεύσας τὸ σωμάτιν ἐλθῖν πρὸς σέ.
>
> Therefore I ask you, my lord, to issue to them a written document so that no one will bother them along the way, so that I may bury the body and come to you.[196]

A party of several men is sent forth to measure some fields, but they can expect to encounter some resistance. Therefore, they carry a letter for someone who will help them to get the business done.

> τοῖς ἀναδιδῶσί σοι ταῦτα μου τὰ γράμματα σύστα πρὸς Ἡρωνᾶṿ ὅπως εὐπιθῆ αὐ[τ]ὲν ποιήσαντες σὺν αὐτοῖς γένῃ ⟦υ⟧ μέχρις ἂν ἀναμετρήσουσ[ι τ]ὰ ἐδάφη.
>
> Assist the persons who are delivering this writing of mine regarding Heronas so that, after you have made him compliant, you may accompany them until they measure the fields.[197]

Collecting a fee for rental can also cause some resistance, which justifies sending a letter of recommendation in support of a farmer.

> Πτῶυς ὁ ἀποδιδούς σοι τὴν ἐπιστολὴν ἔστιν μου ἡμέτερος καὶ Ἀσκληπιάδου ἀντιγραφέως γεωργός· εὖ οὖν ποιήσεις ἐκπράξας τοὺς ὀφ<ε>ίλοντας αὐτῶι ẹị̀ς ẹ̣κ̣φόρια ὧν καταβέβρωκαν <πρόβατα?> αὐτοῦ χλωρὸν [ἴδ]ιον· καὶ γὰρ καὶ αὐτός σοι μετρεῖ τ' ἐκφόρια Ἀσκληπιάδου ἀντιγραφέως· μὴ οὖν ἄλλως [πο]<ι>ή̣σ̣ẹι[ς].
>
> Ptoys who is bringing you this letter is the farmer of myself and Asklepiades, the accountant. Please be so good, therefore, as to collect the rental fees from those persons who owe him for the grass which (their livestock?) have consumed. He himself will measure out to you the rental fees of Asklepiades, the accountant. Do not act contrary to this![198]

---

[195] P.Mich. 8.487.10-15 (II AD), a business letter.

[196] P.Oxy. 7.1068.23-27 (III AD).

[197] P.Mich. 3.210.2-9 (II/III AD).

[198] BGU 16.2654.2-9 (6 BC).

In a brief business note typical of agricultural estates, the sender simply asks the recipient not to bother the bearer of the letter. This occurs again in a letter where the two presumed bearers are looking for work.

> Ἱέραξ ὁ ἀναδιδούς σοι ταῦτά μου τὰ γράμματα μισθωτὴς ἡμῶν ἐγένετο. τοῦτ[ο]ν οὖν μηδὲ ἐνοχλῆς.
>
> Hierax, who is delivering this writing of mine, is our former tenant. Therefore do not make trouble for him.[199]

> καλῶς οὖν ποιήσις παραπροσσχεῖν αὐτοῖς, ἵνα μήτις αὐτοῖς ἐπήριαν ποιήσι.
>
> Please look after them and make sure that nobody creates trouble for them.[200]

4.9.6 Hospitality and accommodation

An individual may need some assistance because he does not know the place where he has landed.

> καλῶς ποήσις ἀποδεξάμενος τὸν κομίζοντά σοι τὸ ἐπιστόλιον (...) ξένος γάρ ἐστιν, καὶ οὐκ οἶδε τοὺς τόπους.
>
> Please receive the person who is bringing this letter to you (...); for he is a stranger and does not know the place.[201]

He may also need a place to stay, which the recipient is asked to provide.

> ἐὰν δὲ δέηται ἐπιξενωθῆναι [. . . . . . .] αὐτὸν ὑποδέξε.
>
> (...) and if he needs your hospitality (...) take him in.[202]

> τόπον δὲ αὐτοῖς παράσχες `αὐτοῖς´ [[μ]] ποῦ μίνωσιν.
>
> Provide them also with a place to stay.[203]

---

[199] SB 4.9439.2-5 (III AD).

[200] P.Gen. 1^2.75.10-13 (III AD).

[201] P.Tebt.Tait 51.5-15 (II/II AD).

[202] P.Oxy. 20.2275.11-12.

[203] P.Gen. 1^2.75.13-15.

> καλῶς οὖν ποιήσεις, ἄδελφε, τοῦτον ὑποδεξάμενος ὡς ἂν ἐμέ. ἀλλὰ καὶ τόπον ἐπειτήδειον αὐτῷ ἀπὸ ποδὸς ἐξηρτισμένον `παράσχες΄, ἀλ<λ>' ἵνα ἐλθὼν μαρτυρήσει μοι τὰ τῆς προαιρέσεώς σου.
>
> Please, brother, receive him as if he were myself. Provide him also with appropriate accommodation, accessibly (?) furnished, making sure that when he comes (to me) he testify to your goodwill.[204]

Another request for accommodation on behalf of the bearer shows how imprecise the boundary between business and family letters can be: this one starts with some detail about the premature birth of a seven-month infant; the real purpose of the message, however, is to secure accommodation for the bearer and several persons accompanying him.

> Ἰναρωοῦς ὁ πατὴρ τῆς μικρᾶς ὁ ἀναδιδούς σοι τὸ ἐπιστόλιον μετὰ Ἀκῆτος τοῦ υἱοῦ Παχοίμιος τοῦ γερδίου καὶ μετὰ καὶ τῶν ἄλλων ἦλθαν εἰς Ὀξυρύγχ(ων) ἀνάγκην αὐτοῖς ἐπιθετεῖ`σ̣΄α̣ν̣ ἐργᾶσθαι ἐν τοῖς τοῦ τιμιωτάτ[ο]υ Ἱερονίκου. εὖ οὖν ποή[σ]εις δώσεις αὐτοῖς τὴν κλῆδα [τῆς] κέλλης τοῦ ἐν τῷ πυλῶνι τη . . [. . . .]κ . . . ικια. λέγει γὰρ Εὐδαιμονὶς ἐφθ̣α̣κέναι παρά σοι ἵνα ἐκεῖ μείνωσι ἕως ἂν λάβωσι ξενίαν ἐκ τοῦ κυρίο̣υ σου.
>
> Inaaroous, the little one's father, who brings this letter to you, together with Akes, son of Pachoimis, the weaver, and also with others, have come to Oxyrhynchos to complete an obligation that was placed upon them in the affairs of the most estimable Hieronikes. Please give them the key to the room of the (…) in the gateway, for Eudaimonis says that they have come first to your side so that they may remain there until they receive hospitality from your lord.[205]

4.9.7 Work and hire

The purpose of the introduction can be to secure some work for the letter's bearer.

> ἔπεμψα πρὸς σὲ Δράκωντα καὶ Μέλανον μισθωτὰς τοῦ κυρίου μου Ἀμβροσίου, εἰσὶν ⟦ρα⟧ γὰρ σκυ⟦θ⟧τεῖς, εἵνα σκυτῇς μετ' αὐτῶν ἕως ἐωνήσαντο κερατέας τῶν ἀγανθέων.
>
> I have sent you Drakon and Melanos, who are day-labourers of my master Ambrosios – for they are tanners – so that you produce leather with them till they have purchased some acacia pods.[206]

A similar situation seems to take place in the following example.

---

[204] P.Oslo 2.55.7-14 (II/III AD).

[205] SB 16.12606.9-22 (III/IV AD; transl. Rowlandson 1998 : 293). Techosous alias Eudaimonis, the woman who is about to give birth, is also known from other documents as a prominent landowner; see Nielsen 1994.

[206] P.Gen. 1^2.75.3-9 (early III AD).

Ἁρπαῆσις [Παπ]ọντῶτος ὁ κομίζων σοι τὴν ἐπιστολήν ἐστιν ὑπογέωργος Θεμιστοκλέους κὰ διὰ σπόρου ζ (ἔτους) ποιῶ αὐτὸν ὑπογέωργον.

Harpaesis son of Papontos, who is bringing this letter to you, is a sub-lessee of Themistokles, and throughout the sowing season of the 7th year, I make him a sub-lessee.[207]

4.10 Conclusion

Carrying the letter constitutes only part of the duties placed in the hands of the bearer. The letter may come with some goods, and more often an item must return to the letter's sender; in both cases, in the absence of the sender, the bearer plays an essential role. Among the numerous tasks assigned to the bearer, by far the most frequent is the conveyance of money back to the sender.

Business letters are often used to introduce the bearer to the recipient, so that he may perform a task on behalf of the sender. Taken together, the cases listed in the above section on letters of recommendation do not provide us with a very consistent picture. Some letters work as short notes of introduction, while in others the sender develops a string of requests. The introduction or recommendation is seldom straightforward: the bearer may be shopping on behalf of the sender while also in need of accommodation; or he should be given some work, and requires also protection from hassle; or the bearer merely represents the sender, who will come later. In all cases, however, the sender seems to engage a portion of his own credit in the action; this empowers the bearer of the letter to ask for the recipient's help. Thus the bearer does not carry only goods, objects or money together with the letter, but also a kind of immaterial currency consisting of the sender's written support.

5 General conclusion

In the complex relationship between the sender and the recipient of a letter, physical distance is clearly the most important factor to be taken into account. Business letters, as opposed to family letters, serve the purpose of getting something done, which the sender cannot achieve personally. Therefore, he must send someone in his stead. A letter does not replace a person completely, but it is often better than nothing at all, in spite of the rhetorical exaggeration found in the following example.

θαυμάζομε[ν] δẹ̀ πῶς Διογένην τὸν σὸν οὐκ ἔπεμ[ψας] π̣ρὸς ἡμᾶς τούτου χάριν, ἀλλὰ ἐπιστ̣[ο]λ̣ειδίῳ̣ ἑ̣νὶ ἠρκέσθης.

We are surprised that you did not send your man Diogenes to us for this purpose, but that you were satisfied with one tiny letter.[208]

[207] P.Oxy. 14.1661.2-7 (AD 74).

[208] PSI 15.1553.9-11 (first half III AD).

This specific mode of communication follows a set of formal rules that can be defined in terms of structure. Some basic elements appear in virtually every business letter; others consist of options, which the sender may activate at will, depending on his business. In addition, some elements occur always in the same part of a business letter, whereas others have no fixed place. Within this structure, the bearer of a letter holds an essential position, even when the sender does not mention him explicitly. He carries some of the competence or prestige of the sender himself. Clearly, in some cases a letter endows the bearer, as the embodiment of the sender, with a kind of symbolic power.

In that respect, our business letters from Roman Egypt pave the way for a metaphor used in letters from the Byzantine period, where the bearer is called an ἔμψυχος ἐπιστολή 'living letter'.

> δέδεξο μετὰ τῆς ἐμψύχου καὶ τὴν ἄψυχον ἐπιστολήν, μετὰ τοῦ θαυμαστοῦ Γεροντίου ταῦτα τὰ γράμματα.
>
> Receive, together with the living letter, also the soulless letter; (i.e.) with the admirable Gerontios, (receive) this writing.[209]

6 Appendix 1: P.Prag. 1.111 revisited

This broad survey of business letters, with a focus on their bearers, allows us to reconsider the edition of one such document, P.Prag. 1.111. There is a general agreement on the fact that we are dealing here with an order to deliver some wine. The detailed process, however, requires clarification.

The interpretation of P.Prag. 1.111 has developed in three successive stages. Rosario Pintaudi, who first edited the text in 1988, encountered a difficulty in lines 12-13 and 20; then Jean Bingen proposed some corrections and a brief interpretation;[210] finally, Dominic Rathbone put forward his own summary interpretation, which differed from Bingen's.[211]

For the sake of clarity, it will be necessary to start with Pintaudi's edition and translation, and then to observe how his text was corrected and interpreted by Bingen and Rathbone. I provide an English version of Pintaudi's Italian translation.

Σιλβανὸς Ἡρω- νείνῳ τῷ φιλ(τάτῳ) χαίρειν. τῷ ἀναδιδόντι σο[ι]	Silvanos to his dearest Heroninos, greetings.

[209] Synes. *Epist.* 85 (IV/V AD).

[210] Bingen 1988 : 376-377.

[211] Rathbone 1991 : 315.

ταῦτά μου τὰ γ[ράμ-]
ματα Ἥρων[ι δὸς]
οἴνου δίχωρ[ον]
ἓν καὶ ἀνερχόμε-
νος κόμισόν μοι
τοῦτο τὸ ἐπιστό-
λιον ἵνα τὴν
τιμὴν μετα-
βάλω̣μ̣α̣ι̣ ***. ση-
[**]*ιου δὲ τούτου
χ̣άριν δέδω-
κάς μοι τὸ σύμ-
βολον τῶν τοῦ
(πυροῦ) (ἀρταβῶν) ιε τῆς
ἀννώνης
ἀλλὰ καλλ(ονὴ) ἤτω
τ̣ὸ οἴνο̣υ̣ δ̣ί̣(χωρον) ἕ̣ν.
(2nd h.) ἐρρῶσθαί σ' εὔχο(μαι)
φίλ̣(τατε).

To Heron, who is delivering to you this message of mine, give a *dichoron* of wine, and on your return, bring along a reply letter, so that I may change the price of the (…); and for that, you have given me the receipt of the 15 *artabai* of wheat of the *annona*. But let the wine *dichoron* be of good quality.

(2nd h.) I pray for your health, my dearest.

Bingen suggested the following corrections.

10-12: ἵνα τὴν τιμὴν μεταβάλω̣μ̣α̣ι̣ *** > ἵνα τὴν τιμὴν μεταβάλω̣μ̣α̣ί̣ σοι. He rightly recognised in μεταβάλωμαι the meaning 'to forward money to another account'; see P.Oxy. 3.532.3-8: ἔδει (…) ἀναπέμψαι τὰς (δραχμὰς) κ, εἰδὼς ὅτι αὐτόθι μετεβαλόμην τοῖς κοινωνοῖς μου αὐτάς 'You should have (…) sent the 20 *drachmai*, knowing that I transferred them here to my partners.' The use of μεταβάλλομαι can also be compared with that of καταβάλλω εἰς λόγον 'to make a payment on an account', see e.g. P.Fay. 63.4-6 (AD 240): κατέβαλ(εν) εἰς τ[ὸν Ἀ]ντωνίνου Φιλοξένου τοῦ [κρ]α̣τίστου λόγον.

12-14: ση[**]*ιου δὲ τούτου χ̣άριν > σημιοῦ δὲ τούτου χάριν. (with a full stop after χάριν). Bingen (377) mentions 'la lettre qu'Hèroninos devra préalablement endosser (σημιοῦ).' Although he offers no translation, his phrasing and his choice of accent imply that he interprets σημιοῦ as a verb in the imperative, 'apply your signature'.

19-20: ἀλλὰ καλλ(ονὴ) ἤτω τ̣ὸ οἴνο̣υ̣ δ̣ί̣(χωρον) ἕ̣ν > ἀλλὰ κάλλ̣[ιον?] ἤτω τὸ οἰνά̣[ρ]ιον. The reading of τὸ οἰνά̣[ρ]ιον seems inescapable. As for the proposed comparative κάλλ̣[ιον], Bingen (377) offers a rough interpretation: 'que ce ne soit pas de la piquette comme la fois précédente!' i.e. 'let this not be second-quality wine like last time!'

Bingen suggests that we are dealing with a kind of cheque: Heroninos is to hand it to Silvanos when he comes to the nome capital; the value of the wine will be recorded in the accounts in exchange for the letter. Then, there is a mention of the *annona*, which he understands as a separate business. To this first interpretation, Rathbone replies by suggesting that the letter corresponds in fact to a sale of wine:

> Another type of sale is possibly attested in P.Prag. 111, in which Silvanus, sending a man whom Heroninos did not know to collect some wine, wrote as proof of his authorship of the letter 'you have given me the receipt (*sumbolon*) for the 15 art. wheat of the *annona*' (from the plate I read ll. 12-13 as μεταβάḷωμαί σοι. σημίου δὲ τούτου χ̣άρ̣ιν = 'As proof of this...'; I do not agree with the interpretation of J. Bingen (...)). The 'proof' may have been a pre-agreeed fiction; possibly, however, Heroninos had paid in 15 *art.* as tax on Silvanus' account for which Silvanus was to pay him.[212]

Rathbone correctly recognised in σημ<ε>ίου a noun. The expression σημείου χάριν 'as way of proof' normally introduces the mention of an element of which only the sender and the recipient of the letter have knowledge; it is used as a way of authenticating a letter, as we have seen above.[213]

It appears that both scholars got some points right. We should proceed further by solving one last difficulty in the reading of the papyrus, before attempting to bridge the conflicting interpretations of Bingen and Rathbone. In line 19, the published image does not seem to allow room for ἀλλὰ κάλλ̣[ιον?] ἤτω τὸ οἰνά̣[ρ]ιον: the available space suggests rather ἀλλὰ καλο̣ν̣ ἤτω τὸ οἰνά̣[ρ]ιον.[214]

The corrected text should thus run as follows:

Σιλβανὸς Ἡρω-
νείνῳ τῷ φιλ(τάτῳ) χαίρειν.
τῷ ἀναδιδόντι σο[ι]
ταῦτά μου τὰ γ[ράμ-]
ματα Ἥρων̣[ι δὸς]
οἴνου δίχωρ[ον]
ἓν καὶ ἀνερχόμε-
νος κόμισόν μοι
τοῦτο τὸ ἐπιστό-
λιον ἵνα τὴν
τιμὴν μετα-

Silvanos to his dearest Heroninos, greetings. To Heron, who is delivering to you this message of mine, give a *dichoron* of wine; and when you come back (to me), bring this letter so that I may transfer the value (of the wine) onto your account. As way of proof of this (i.e. of the

[212] Rathbone 1991 : 315, n. 70.

[213] Youtie 1970; above, σημεῖον clause.

[214] In the Heroninos archive, see P.Flor. 2.166.5: ἀλλὰ ἤτω ὁ χοῖρος καλός 'but let it be a good pig'; P.Flor. 2.175.8-9: ἀλλὰ ἤτω ἐπειτήδιος (l. ἐπιτήδειος) 'but let him be appropriate'. The imperative ἤτω appears in our documents in the late second or early third cent. AD; see Mandilaras 1973 : 79, § 118; 292, § 682.

βάλω̣μ̣α̣ί̣ σοι.
σημίου δὲ τούτου
χ̣άριν· δέδω-
κάς μοι τὸ σύμ-
βολον τῶν τοῦ
(πυροῦ) (ἀρταβῶν) ιε τῆς
ἀννώνης. ἀλλὰ καλ̣ὸ̣ν̣ ἤτω
τ̣ὸ οἰνά̣[ρ]ιον.
(2nd h.) ἐρρῶσθαί σ' εὔχο(μαι)
φί̣λ̣(τατε).

authenticity of my order): you gave me the receipt for the 15 *artabai* of the *annona*. By the way, let the wine be of good quality. (2nd hand, presumably that of Silvanos) I pray for your health, my dearest.

It now becomes possible to reconstruct the short story described in this document. Heron – whom Heroninos does not know personally – is carrying a letter from Silvanos. When Heroninos receives it, he should give some wine to Heron and keep the letter as a receipt for the wine he gave out. Later, he is expected to meet Silvanos and hand him the letter back; in exchange, Silvanos will credit Heroninos for the wine in the book of accounts.

There is a risk, however, that a stranger could come to Heroninos and claim some wine with a fake letter. Silvanos, upon receiving the letter in return from Heroninos, would declare that he never issued the order in the first place. As Rathbone correctly understood, this explains the mention of the *annona*, an event that is not directly related to the present business – Bingen was right on that – but serves as a code of recognition between the sender and the recipient (12-14: σημ<ε>ίου δὲ τούτου χ̣άριν).

Bingen correctly described this letter as a cheque. Until Heroninos hands the letter back to Silvanos, his account will display a loss of one *dichoron*; Silvanos will transfer (10-12: ἵνα τὴν τιμὴν μεταβάλω̣μ̣α̣ί̣ σοι) a corresponding credit when he gets the letter back. Silvanos has not fixed the price for the wine. Likewise, when on another occasion Heroninos writes to his son Heronas, he asks him to give a certain amount of wine to the bearer of the letter λαβὼν παρ' αὐτοῦ ὃ <ἐ>ὰν δωση σοι κέρμα 'accepting whatever money he will give you'.[215] He also adds a note at the end of the message (11-12): ἐὰν δὲ ἄλω γομάριν θέλωσιν δὸς αὐτοῖς λαβὼν τὴν τειμ̣ή̣ν̣ 'if they want another load of wine, give it to them and take the price (for it)'.

As a short case study, the revision of P.Prag. 1.111 provides a confirmation of several elements that were described above, in particular the role of the letter's bearer, the token of identification, and the importance of the bearer in the virtual transfer of money.

[215] P.Flor. 2.274.7-9.

7 Appendix 2: proposed corrections to papyri

- BGU 3.829.6-7: καὶ ἐ̣[ν]τ̣[άχιο]ν θέλει ὁ κομίζων `σοι τὸ̣´ διο[ρ]θῶσε̣ τὸ ὑπόμνημα. Correct to: καὶ ἐ̣[π]ι̣γ[νοὺς] τ̣ί θέλει ὁ κομίζων {`σοι τὸ̣ <ὑπόμνημα>´}, διο[ρ]θῶσε̣ τὸ ὑπόμνημα. See Schubert 2018a.
- P.Laur. 3.102 verso.10-11: ἔπεμψα διὰ τοῦ [ἐπιδιδόν]τος. Correct to: ἔπεμψα διὰ τοῦ [ἀναδιδόν]τος.
- P.Prag. 1.111: see Appendix 1.
- P.Stras. 4.174.5-6: σ[υ]ν[π]ά|θητε. Correct to συ̣ν̣έ̣λ|θητ̣ε.
- P.Vars. 23.4: οὐκ ἂν ἐδοκεν. Correct to: οὐκ ἀνέδοκεν (i.e. ἀνέδωκεν).

8 Bibliography

All papyri are quoted after the *Checklist of Editions* <http://papyri.info/docs/checklist>.

- Adams, C. (2007), *Land transport in Roman Egypt. A study in economics and administration in a Roman province* (Oxford).
- Bagnall, R.S. & Cribiore, R. (2006), *Women's letters from ancient Egypt 300 BC – AD 800* (Ann Arbor).
- Bianchi, A. (1983), 'Aspetti della politica economico-fiscale di Filippo l'Arabo', *Aegyptus* 63 : 185–198.
- Bingen, J. (1988), 'Hèroninos, Théadelphie et son vin', *Chronique d'Égypte* 63 : 367–378.
- Blumell, L.H. (2011), 'A second-century AD letter of introduction in the Washington State University Collection', *Tyche* 26 : 33–39.
- Blumell, L.H. (2014), 'The message and the medium: some observations on epistolary communication in Late Antiquity', *Journal of Greco-Roman Christianity and Judaism* 10 : 24–67.
- Ceccarelli, P. (2013), *Ancient Greek letter writing: a cultural history (600 BC-150 BC)* (Oxford).
- Cuvigny, H. (2005), *Ostraca de Krokodilô. La correspondance militaire et sa circulation* (*Fouilles de l'IFAO* 51, Le Caire).
- Cuvigny, H. (2019), 'Le livre de poste de Turbo, curateur du *praesidium* de Xèron Pelagos', in Kolb, A. (ed.), *Roman roads. New evidence, new perspectives* (Berlin & Boston) : 67–106.
- Daniel, R.W. (1984), 'Through straying streets: a note on σημασία-texts', *Zeitschrift für Papyrologie und Epigraphik* 54 : 85–86.
- Daris, S. (1991), *Il lessico latino nel greco d'Egitto* (2nd ed., Barcelona).
- Drexhage, H.-J. (1989), 'Zu den Überstellungsbefehlen aus dem römischen Ägypten (1.-3. Jahrhundert n.Chr.)', in Drexhage, H.-J. & Sünskes, J. (ed.), *Migratio et commutatio. Studien zur Alten Geschichte und deren Nachleben Thomas Pekáry dargebracht* (St. Katharinen) : 102–118.
- Exler, F.X.J. (1923), *The form of the ancient Greek letter. A study in Greek epistolography* (Catholic University of America).

- Fowler, D.P. (1985), 'New Directions', *Zeitschrift für Papyrologie und Epigraphik* 59 : 45–46.
- Gagos, T. & Sijpesteijn, P.J. (1996), 'Towards an explanation of the typology of the so-called 'orders to arrest'', *Bulletin of the American Society of Papyrologists* 33 : 77–97.
- Gascou, J. (2012), 'La σημασία P.Oxy. XXXIV 2719 et le paysage urbain d'Alexandrie', *Chronique d'Égypte* 87 : 308–318.
- Hagedorn, D. (2001), 'Bemerkungen zu Urkunden', *Zeitschrift für Papyrologie und Epigraphik* 136 : 148–154.
- Hagedorn, U. (1979), 'Das Formular der Überstellungsbefehle im Römischen Ägypten', *Bulletin of the American Society of Papyrologists* 16 (1979) 61–74.
- Head, P.M. (2009), 'Named letter-carriers among the Oxyrhynchus papyri', *Journal for the Study of the New Testament* 31 : 279–300.
- Huss, W. (2011), *Die Verwaltung des ptolemaiischen Reichs* (*Münchner Beiträge zur Papyrusforschung und antiken Rechtsgeschichte* 104, München).
- Keyes, C.W. (1935), 'The Greek letter of introduction', *American Journal of Philology* 56 : 28–44.
- Kim, Ch.-H. (1972), *The familiar letter of recommendation* (*Society of Biblical Literature Dissertation Series* 4, Missoula).
- Kolb, A. (2000), *Transport und Nachrichtentransfer im Römischen Reich* (Berlin).
- Koskenniemi, H. (1956), *Studien zu Idee und Phraseologie des griechischen Briefes bis 400 n. Chr.* (Helsinki).
- Lewis, N. (1997), *The compulsory public services of Roman Egypt* (*Papyrologica Florentina* 28, 2nd ed., Firenze).
- Llewelyn, S.R. (1994), 'The function of the σημασία-texts, P.Oxy. XXXIV 2719 and SB XVI 12550', *Zeitschrift für Papyrologie und Epigraphik* 104 : 230–232.
- Mandilaras, B.G. (1973), *The verb in the Greek non-literary papyri* (Athens).
- Nielsen, B.E. (1994), 'A woman of property: Tachosous alias Eudaimonis', *Bulletin of the American Society of Papyrologists* 31 : 129–136.
- Parsons, P.J. (1967), 'Philippus Arabs and Egypt', *Journal of Roman Studies* 57 : 134–141.
- Rathbone, D. (1991), *Economic rationalism and rural society in third-century A.D. Egypt* (Cambridge).
- Rowlandson, J. (ed.) (1998), *Women and society in Greek and Roman Egypt. A sourcebook* (Cambridge).
- Russo, S. (2004), *Le calzature nei papiri di età greco-romana* (*Studi e Testi di Papirologia* N.S. 2, Firenze).
- Sarri, A. (2018), *Material aspects of letter writing in the Graeco-Roman world* (Berlin & Boston).
- Schubert, P. (2018a), 'BGU III 829: une lettre du préfet Gaius Vibius Maximus', *Chronique d'Égypte* 93 : 130–144.
- Schubert, P. (2018b), 'Warrants: some further considerations on their typology', *Bulletin of the American Society of Papyrologists* 55 : 253-274.
- Steen, H.A. (1938), 'Les clichés épistolaires dans les lettres sur papyrus grecques', *Classica et Mediaevalia* 1 : 119-176.

- Vandorpe, K. (1996), 'Seals in and on papyri of Greco-Roman and Byzantine Egypt', in Boussac, M.-F. & Invernizzi, A. (edd.), *Archives et sceaux du monde hellénistique* (BCH Suppl. 29, Athens) : 231–291.
- Visser, E. (1935), 'Briefe und Urkunden aus der Berliner Papyrussammlung', *Aegyptus* 15 : 267–276.
- White, J.L. (1972), *The form and function of the body of the Greek letter* (Missoula MT).
- Youtie, H.C. (1970), 'ΣΗΜΕΙΟΝ in the papyri and its significance for Plato, *Epistle* 13 (360a-b)', *Zeitschrift für Papyrologie und Epigraphik* 6 : 105–116 [= *Scriptiunculae* II 963–975].

9 Indices

9.1 Papyri

9.2 Other ancient sources

9.3 Place names

9.4 Greek words

9.5 General index